Library of Congress
Catalogue Number:
89-61571

Hardcover ISBN:
0-917631-07-2

Printed by Mobility Inc.
Richmond, Virginia.

Produced and distributed
by Lightworks,
6005 Chapel Hill Road,
Raleigh, N.C. 27607.
Telephone (919) 851-0518
or (800) 334-3296.

THE BIG CLICK

Photographs Of One Day
In North Carolina

April 21, 1989

6:30 pm
Set back among the sand dunes, the old Coast Guard cottages stand guard over the tip of Bald Head Island, the Frying Pan Shoals and East Beach.

Jim Moriarty

THE BIG CLICK

*Photographs Of One Day
In North Carolina*

April 21, 1989

Sponsors

American Airlines,
*Southeastern
Regional Office,
Research Triangle Park*

Capitol Broadcasting
Company, Inc., *Raleigh*

Henderson, Collins &
Muir, Inc., *Raleigh*

Mobility, Inc.,
Richmond, VA

JW Photo Labs, *Raleigh*

11:45 p.m., April 19, Raleigh, N.C.–Chip Henderson hasn't slept much in the last few days. Near the countdown, he drinks Pepsi and talks about THE BIG CLICK. It's a project some would call mammoth, radical, impossible. For two years, he's called it his dream.

"In twenty-four hours, all the planning, prayer and hard work will come together.

"Over 240 photographers will load their cameras and fan out across the state to document it for one entire day. If it rains on the 21st, we could lose our publishing business, we've risked that much on this venture.

"But I have peace about the weather. The date wasn't something we arbitrarily pulled out of the air.

"Late last summer, I decided to go ahead and put together a state-wide photography event in North Carolina.

"We wanted to record, from midnight to midnight, the beauty, the splendor, the grace of the people and the place.

"We contacted hundreds of photographers: the American

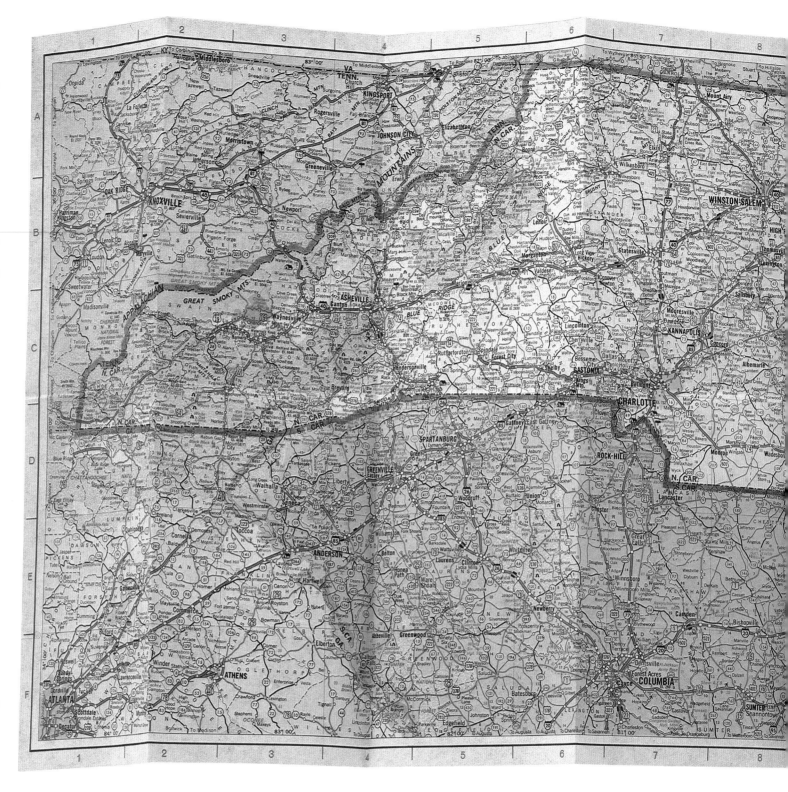

North Carolina Road Map 1989
by Rand McNally & Company, R.L. 89-S-86

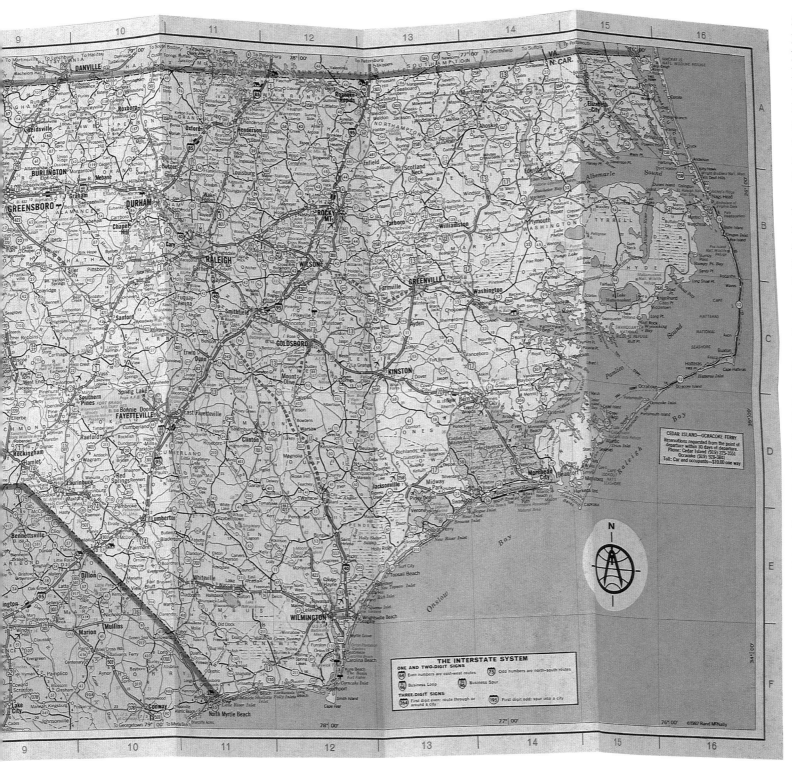

Society of Magazine Photographers, the North Carolina Press Photographers Association, the Professional Photographers of North Carolina. Anyone who was a working photographer was invited to join in this adventure.

"One thing that kept us going when the money was running low and sponsors were hard to find, was their enthusiasm. It was unbelievably contagious.

"On April 21, BIG CLICK photographers will be underneath the Graveyard of the Atlantic, photographing a wreck. They'll be hanging out of airplanes and helicopters. They'll be on a llama farm, on military bases, at church suppers, everywhere.

"We've given out 4,000 rolls of film. We've worked with the photojournalism school at UNC. We've planned, coordinated, toured, advertised, promoted, spent, lost sleep and kept the faith. There's nothing else we can do."

Except sit and watch the western sky.

Will the high pressure system move through North Carolina, push the low pressure out and give

2:00 pm
On Bald Head Island, Anne Newmann Potter from Auroa, IL, stoops to get a close-up of the dune grass bending in the breeze off the Cape Fear River.

us fair weather?

"It's not really a picture book as much as it is a history book. Fifty years from now, I hope people will wonder, what did they wear? How did they live? What were they like? And they can look at this book and find out."

Chip Henderson pauses awhile, then says soberly: "If…it doesn't rain."

On the day of the event, North Carolina weather was spectacular.

Great cumulus clouds moved across majestic sweeps of blue sky.

Sunrises and sunsets were breathtaking from Manteo to Murphy, streaking the heavens with lavendar and crimson, platinum and gold.

Five days after the event, thousands of rolls of film had come in.

From the initial edit to the final, tough-minded category the judges called Select, the work was solid, ambitious, exciting, and sometimes, even breakthrough.

A noted North Carolina photographer wrote Chip Henderson to say, "I can't think of many things I've done in the last few years that meant as much to me as being part of 'THE BIG CLICK'."

One of the early books released by Henderson's publishing company was "North Carolina: A Blessing Shared."

We believe this book shares an even greater blessing.

Jan Karon
Blowing Rock, NC

12:15 am

Many children dream of becoming doctors, lawyers and policemen, but a fire fighter has the best job in the world, according to Jerry Fitzgerald, a member of Elizabeth City Fire Department's Station No. 1. "The fire fighters complete their 24-hour shifts at 8:00 A.M.," said Fitzgerald, "but only if they're lucky; most calls occur between midnight and 7:00 A.M.," he said.

Jim Colman

12:15 am
What is a late hour to some is an early time to BIG CLICK photographer Charles Ledford who has come from Florida to photograph some of the Ledfords who still live in the tiny communities of Clay County in western North Carolina.

Charles Ledford

12:05 am

Mike Hervey, 22, has been a police officer for four years in Charlotte. His comments: "I like excitement and there is a lot of job satisfaction. You are pretty much your own boss; you control what you do out here on the street, but you are responsible for the decisions you make. I just don't want to do anything else. I just feel lucky."

Henry Mills

12:25 am
In Raleigh, News and Observer *copy editor Bill Dupre picks up copy for the final edition of the April 21st newspaper and heads back to his Coyote computer terminal to make any last minute changes to copy.*

Roger Winstead

8

12:55 am
 Police officers E.W. Earp (left) and D.A. Proctor make their midnight rounds checking doors along Fayetteville Street Mall in downtown Raleigh. So far the only noise has been an alarm at a downtown church set off by a pair of street people while trying to sleep in the bushes close by.

Roger Winstead

3:30 am
Big rigger, Alan Carde, at the Petro City Truck Stop off S.R. Highway 85 en route to Hillsborough.

Janet Jarman

4:30 am
AFC-E3 Christopher L. Phelps of Newport, NC, and his sentry-trained dog named Pluto on duty at Seymour Johnson Air Force Base.

Roger Ball

5:20 am
Sunlight has not yet broken on the rain-wet docks in Wilmington. "Trade Light" from Panama waits to be off-loaded.

Paul Nurnberg

15

5:45 am
*On a productive
peach and cattle farm in
the Sandhills, it is not
uncommon to find Watts
Aumen beginning a long
day with a cup of coffee.*

Herman Lankford

5:15 am

Powerful antennae at The Edward R. Murrow Transmitting Station of Voice of America, Greenville, transmit commentary, music, and new programs to countries in 31 languages. Greenville is the largest transmitting facility of VOA, which is a part of the U.S. Information Agency. Says Bob Sutton, shift supervisor of operations, "There are things that happen in this country that we should be ashamed of, but if we don't tell the whole truth to the world, they can't believe us. We have to maintain our credibility. That's one of our purposes—to tell the truth."

Brian Whittier

5:50 am
While first light still permits a range of royal colors, the men and women of the U.S. Army Parachute Team called Golden Knights board their FK-27 "Friendship" aircraft at Ft. Bragg.

Sgt. Joe Belcher

6:00 am
A fisherman works on his nets on Perquimans River.

Mark Sluder

6:15 am
Transmission lines carry electricity from the Roxboro Electric Plant to thousands of customers of Carolina Power and Light Company.

Peter Damroth

6:00 am
At Frank A. Jessup Country Store in Westfield, north of Kernersville, Frank Jessup continues much as he has for 55 years. "I am 80 years old, and I open every morning at 6:00 A.M. I've lived here all my life. It's the best place in the world," he says.

Jim Koch

6:00 am
Bernard McCullough (yellow slicker) of Bayboro and Howard Lee Jones of Vandermere take in nets on the "Miss Key" troller on Pamlico Sound near Oriental.

Larry Ketchum

6:30 am
It's a goodbye kiss for mom (Beverly Cauble of Salisbury) from Misty Williams, 9, as she leaves for a babysitter's house on a day when Rowan County Schools are enjoying Spring Break.

Charles Gupton

6:00 am
   Clarence Hamilton, from Salisbury, NC, has been with the Great American Circus for several years. He sets up bleachers under the Big Top, a daily job and a tough one.

Pam Royal

6:20 am
In a Clay County community, Manuel Blankenship sits at the breakfast table while his wife Josephine packs his lunch to take to his job, house building.

Charles Ledford

6:15 am

John Bateman, a student at East Carolina University and Marine reservist, pays tribute to the men and women who lost their lives during the Vietnam War. More than 206,000 North Carolinians were among those who served in that war; nearly 1,600 men and 1 woman from the state died as a result of it. He kneels at a half-scale replica of the permanent Vietnam Veterans Memorial in Washington, D.C. This memorial, called the Moving Wall, was assembled and displayed at the Town Commons, Greenville, on April 14 through April 21.

Billy Walls

6:30 am
The morning line-up for milking outside North Carolina State University College of Veterinary Medicine in Raleigh.

Kenneth Martin

6:15 am
As the first rays of sunshine pierce the woods in Chatham County, Ed Alston, fully camouflaged, uses a red cedar box turkey call to entice a wild tom turkey to the gun. But on April 21, no tom turkeys answer the call.

Terry Shankle

6:35 am
A hazy, colorful early day near North Wilkesboro.

Steve Murray

6:35 am
Left from the previous day's work and maybe needed on this new day are jeans and work clothes on a clothesline in Piney Green near Clinton.

Tory Chisholm

6:45 am

R.C. Cole, of the North Carolina Forestry Service of the Great Smoky Mountains, has an extensive view atop Toxaway fire tower. He says that sunny, windy days can bring fires. "When you have a big fire agoin' and the planes and helicopters are bringing chemicals in, then that's a real fire," he says.

Chip Henderson

6:45 am

"Thank You, Lord, for this day and for making it possible for us to get into the fields for the first time today." James Earl Flythe, Sr., expresses gratitude shared by many farmers in Northampton County and across the state in a time when late snows and heavy rains have hindered plowing and seriously interrupted crop production. If there is a typical farm family in North Carolina, perhaps this is it. The Flythes work 1200 acres of peanuts, corn, soybeans and cotton. They share breakfast together before sharing the demanding work of each day. At left and rotating clockwise: son James Earl Flythe, Jr.; Terry Britton, a family friend who works with the Flythes during crop season; son Keith "Chick" Flythe; wife Virginia and Earl Flythe. On this morning a third son, William, and his wife, Sandra, both of whom operate tractors on the farm, are at home with their child who is not feeling well.

Nat Felts

6:45 am
Physical fitness, including running in formation on Ardennes St., is one of the main activities each day for the men and women of the 82nd Airborne Division of the U.S. Army based at Fort Bragg.

Ken Cooke

7:00 am
David and Tim Disher in Lewisville in western Forsyth County, farm 300 acres owned by their grandfather, and lease additional land from neighbors. Dairyman David (left), 23, says,"You have to love farming; otherwise you couldn't put up with it."

Bill Ray

7:00 am
An unidentified man walks past the County Courthouse in Wilson, unaware that anyone is close by.

Brian Whittier

7:00 am
  The "Old Winchester Place" at dawn. The house is about 100 years old, and was built about the time that Clay became an independent county. It now sits in the middle of a cow pasture in Tusquittee.

Charles Ledford

7:10 am
  On the way to Hickory by air – an incredibly beautiful morning.

Steve Murray

7:15 am
Morning mist at Castle Bridge on Lake Rhodhiss in Caldwell County.

Peter Sawyer

7:15 am
	Odell Artis, 70, from Saratoga near Wilson, is a bus washer and has been with Carolina America Charter Tours for 20 years. "I'd rather do a bus than a car."

Brian Whittier

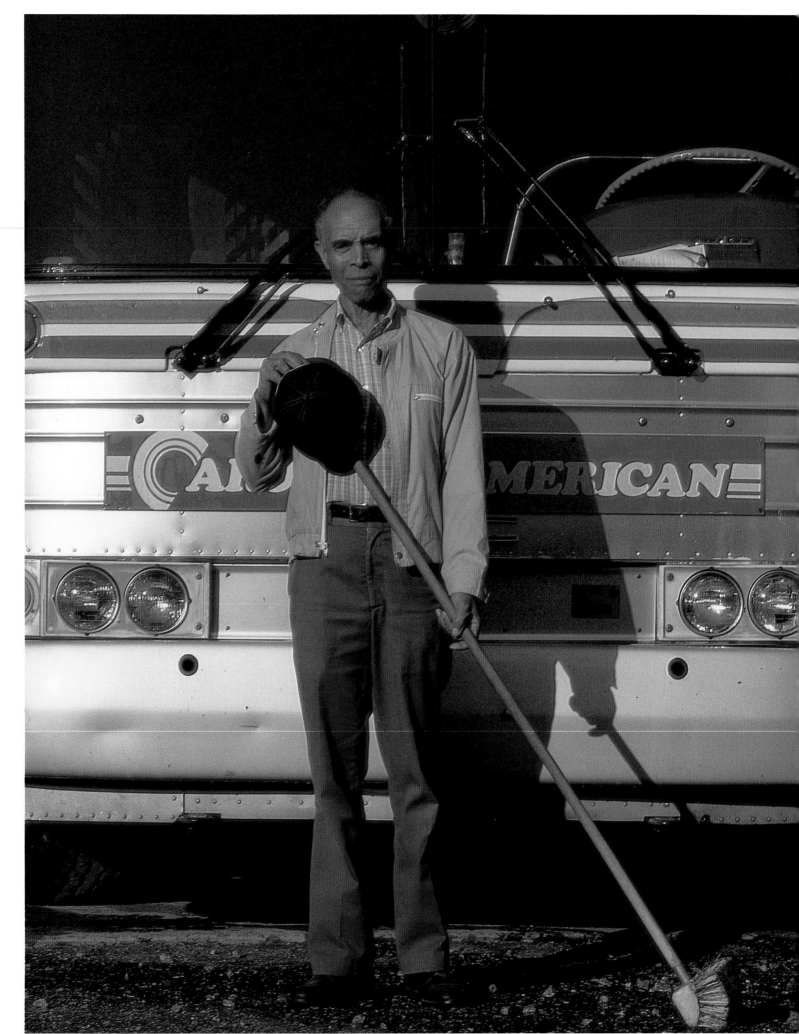

7:20 am
  Chef and owner, Bill Piscatello, at work at his Breadman's Restaurant in Chapel Hill.

Cliff Haac

7:28 am
    Molly Levin, 11,
considers the morning.
She is the photographer's
daughter, and attends
South Toe Elementary
School in Celo, Yancey
County.

Wanda Levin

7:30 am
Farmlands on the New River form pleasant patterns in western North Carolina.

Steve Murray

7:45 am
Bobby Carroll, a town of Warwaw employee who has lived in the Western Duplin County town all his life, mows grass beside the railroad tracks downtown.

Mike Collins

7:45 am
Mr. and Mrs. Allison, Old Fort, are following a ritual: each day for two years they have traveled to Black Mountain to have breakfast at Hardee's.

John Warner

7:30 am

Tracy Parris, general manager of Mast General Store in the western town of Valle Crucis, doubles as postmaster in the store's post office. "We keep 140 boxes full and have a waiting list, because of the valley's growth. Not a bad deal–box rental for $2.00 per year."

Neil Sander

7:40am
A waitress picks up breakfast orders from the short order cook at City View Restaurant, popular spot for the first meal of the day in Salisbury. It is owned by Tad Fricke, whose father ran a furniture store there for 38 years prior to City View's opening five years ago.

Charles Gupton

7:40 am
   Naval ROTC Midshipman Tom Liverance was among others on the campus of the University of North Carolina preparing to raise the flag on April 21. Throughout the nation that day, on campuses and at public and private institutions, the United States flag would fly at half mast in remembrance of sailors killed on the U.S.S. Iowa.

Scott Sharpe

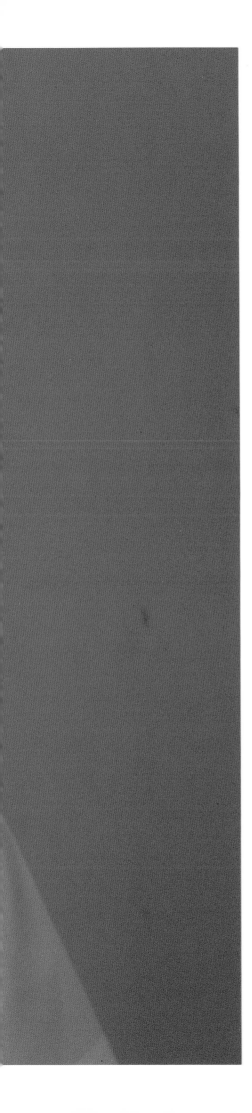

7:45 am

High on a mountain in a remote section of the reservation, a Cherokee Indian named Ed Welch farms alone for his food. He has no car or tractor, nor close neighbors. A few months ago his horse "ole Joe" died, leaving Ed alone to scrape a living out of the earth. "Planting use to be a lot easier when 'ole Joe' was around. But God has been mighty good to me, I still have potatoes and corn in the barn." He built the log barn alone by hand.

Duane Hall

8:00 am

Tim Frisco is the elephant trainer for the Great American Circus and the only man that this elephant obeys. Janet is one of two elephants that travel with the circus. Although it is rare now, the Great American Circus uses elephants to raise and lower the Big Top. In Clinton on this date, the circus performs in a different town each day for 265 consecutive days.

Pam Royal

8:00 am

Silhouette of pilot Chip Parks inside "The Spirit of Kitty Hawk," official balloon of the state of North Carolina.

Will & Deni McIntyre

8:15 am
*This tray is filled
with soft-shell crabs,
surrounded by hay.
Refrigerated trucks
from the north pick up
the packed crabs and
deliver them directly to
market. Mark and Penny
Hooper of Smyrna are
proprietors.*

Scott Taylor

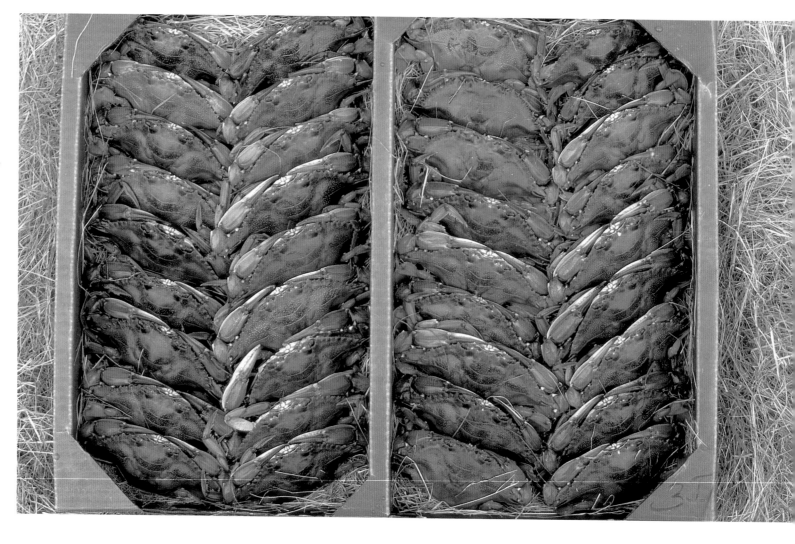

8:00 am
At Hooper Family Seafood, Smyrna, gloves dangle on a line. They serve as protection in handling live crabs to ship to New York City.

Scott Taylor

8:00 am
An old ginning mill in Weeksville, not now operational, casts its reflection in the water below.

Mark Sluder

8:00 am

Bud Pollard is oil and maintenance supervisor for Edgecombe County. Once a month he checks the four faces and motor of the 1887 clock in the Tarboro Clock Tower above Edgecombe County Courthouse, a job he has had for 15 years. Getting this shot was not easy for the photographer. "It was a tight and steep climb. There was a point where I had to hand my camera and bag to the guy in front of me," he said referring to the 40 or 45-foot climb straight up the ladder.

Bill Goode

8:05 am
A croquet player in handsome whites at Pinehurst Country Club.

Charles Register

8:20 am
    A minister's warm greeting and a touch of history enhance a visit to historic Bath and St. Thomas Episcopal Church, the oldest church structure in the state.

Ronny Borton

8:15 am
An American Airlines ground worker gives instructions to pilot about pulling out at Raleigh-Durham International Airport.

Jon Silla

8:30 am
    *Theodore (Ted)
Mutro, crew member of
the "Carteret" ferry from
Ocracoke to Swan
Quarter reads of the
explosion on the U.S.S.
Iowa, in which 47 crew
members were killed.*

Mark Fortenberry

8:10 am
Preparing for classes at UNC, freshman David Woodell in Connor dorm's bathroom.

Scott Sharpe

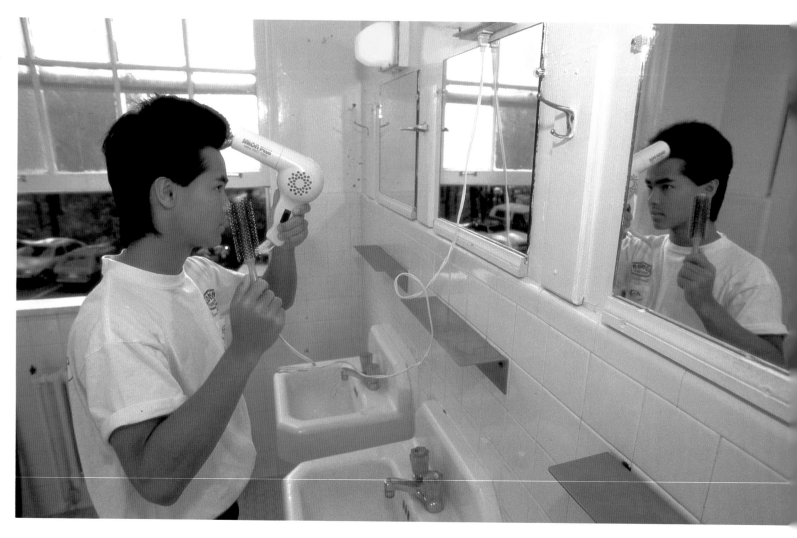

8:32 am
   "When they come out of Jones Barber Shop, they should look good enough to be models for GQ," says Richard Bowden, manager, and he gives this present customer his best work.

Talib Sabir-Calloway

8:27am
Airman First Class Larsen of the Aircraft Maintenance Unit of Seymour Johnson Air Force Base conducts cleaning chores on an F-4 Phantom jet.

Roger Ball

8:32 am
At East Harper School in Lenoir, students get a lesson in the history of the American flag, and an opportunity to show their talents.

David Rufty

8:35 am

Push-ups are light discipline for these cadets at Oak Ridge Military Academy in Guilford County, the last such institution left in North Carolina, and one registered as a National Historic District.

Robert Cavin

9:00am

John Cooper of Newland, a 78-year-old mountain man who helped construct the Blue Ridge Parkway between Asheville and Mt. Mitchell, was in for a sad surprise on April 21. On the Mt. Mitchell Balsam Nature Trail near the 6,684-ft. summit, a region he has not visited since his work on the Parkway there 40 years prior, he found dead timber everywhere. The destruction is due in part, at least, to acid rain. The rings of this dead spruce, that had been sawed when the dead trees were blown down in the trail, reveal much. The trees had robust, healthy growth in early years, but the rings at the outside edge of the trunk are extremely thin, representing virtually no timber growth in the recent years when acid rain has placed great stress on the trees at this location.

Hugh Morton

8:50 am
    George "Sharkman"
Lockhart, a fourth
generation fisherman in
the Carteret County area,
examines a shark jaw for
teeth that can be made
into marketable jewelry
for Atlantic Beach and
Morehead City
waterfront shops.

John Geis

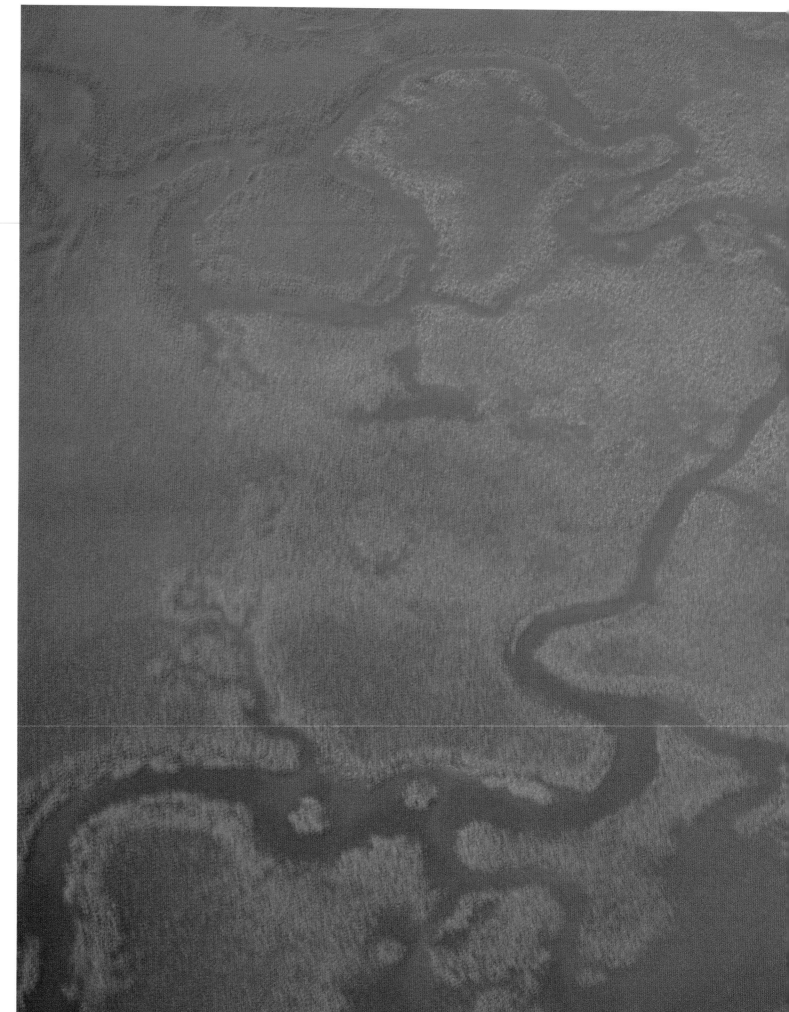

9:00am
This was the view of salt water marshes on Bald Head Island approximately 1,000 feet overhead in an airplane. The flock of small white aquatic birds flying by was an added attraction.

Cramer Gallimore

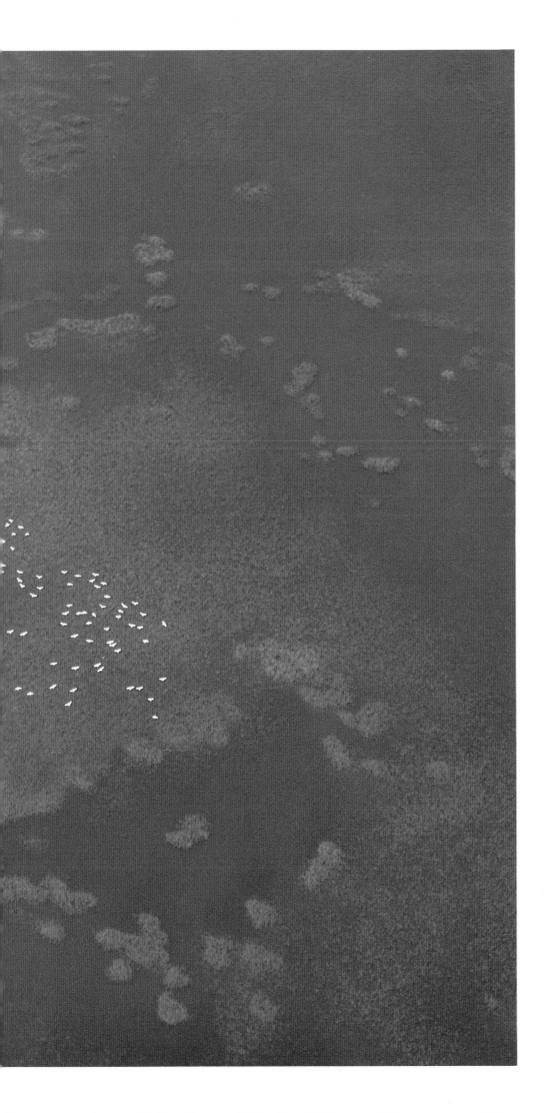

9:00 am

Nervous tension fills the air as members of the naval junior ROTC unit at John A. Holmes High School in Edenton, stand at attention. April 21 is the day scheduled for the group's annual inspection by a regular navy officer from the Norfolk Naval Base. Captain C.A. Futch, NJROTC area manager five, conducted the morning inspection.

Jim Colman

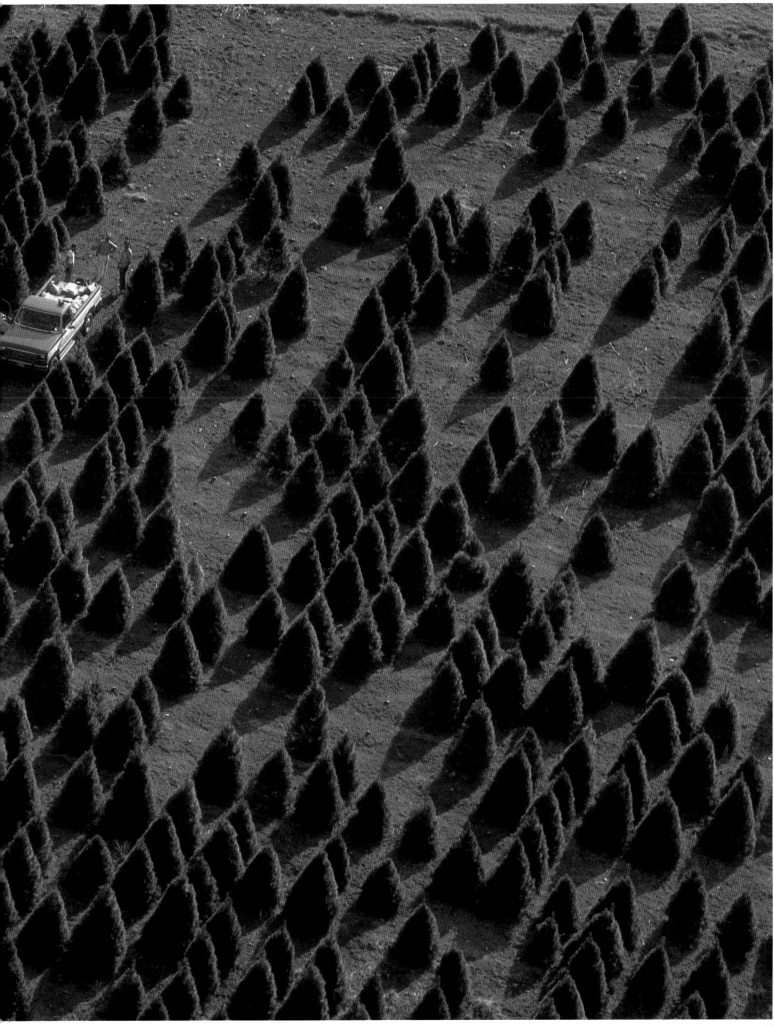

9:12 am
Christmas tree farm off the New River in northwestern North Carolina.

Steve Murray

9:30 am

Willie Johnson,
a 12-year veteran of
Burlington Industries,
watches as 11,088 strands
of polyester are unrolled.
Willie is a slasher helper:
he looks for breaks in the
yarn as 400 yards speed
by every minute. "If even
one strand breaks, I stop
it all and retie it," he says.
He is at the Richmond
Plant in Cordova.

Curtis Myers

9:20 am
*Kathrin Weber Scott,
handweaver, devotes
time and skill to creating
useful and decorative
tablecloths, bed throws,
and many other fiber
items at the Craft Guild
of Western North
Carolina in Clyde.*

Jim Mosley

9:30 am
    C.E. Tomlinson of
Smithfield coaxes a little
kiss from Bolero's Bandit,
one of seven horses that
he boards in an old mule
barn on his farm. The
barn, built in 1835 of
longleaf pine and oak, is
on land that has belonged
to the Tomlinson clan
since the late 1700s.

Calvin Edgerton

9:30 am

Queenie Jackson of Kinston, a personable and resourceful lady, takes care of her flowers; grows potatoes, tomatoes, carrots, beets, greens, lettuce, radishes and corn from her own seed; makes yard decorations such as bird baths from clay pots and garbage can lids; does all her own painting, and puts in a sidewalk or new fence posts as needed.

Charles Buchanan

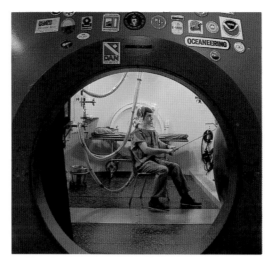

9:30 am
    Research is conducted in the hyperbaric environmental laboratory at Duke Medical Center where conditions match those of NASA test personnel.

Jeff Collidge

9:45 am
    Bennie Gordon operates a carving machine that duplicates furniture legs from a master at Councill Craftsmen manufacturer in Denton.

Bob Heist

9:45 am

At Papa Len's Catch of the Sea restaurant in Waynesville, owner Allan Costa, a veteran in the business, prepares for lunch customers. The menu is Italian as well as seafood, cooked and served in a 70x12–foot trailer that Allan says was dubbed 'ugly blue' by a local newspaper. The reference had the effect of inspiring more customers; so rather than try to create the appearance of a boat as originally planned, Allan and his wife, Marilyn, kept their trailer just as it was.

Julie Stovall

9:30 am

   Bill Lamonds may be called a folk artist, a wood carver, a master toymaker or just a laid-back character; to those who know him, Bill's a North Carolina legend. In his studio, located miles from nowhere, back in the deep woods of north-west Moore County, Bill works diligently, producing toys for children. He says, "I try to make my toys to last almost forever–at least to the next generation so they can have a little fun, too…."

Richard A. Petty

9:45 am

James Bowman who lives in Climax, North Carolina, heads up Red Cross/Randleman Road on his daily walk of a couple of miles. When asked his age, he responded, "I'm 92; I ain't young." Bowman said he was raised on a farm and had lived on one all of his life.

Jerry Wolford

9:45 am
Since she was accustomed to feeding her chickens from hand to mouth on her Ronda farm, Jennie Wright was ready to try it with these seagulls at Atlantic Beach. Soon, though, she discovered that their flapping wings can be scary up close. Jennie and her family began feeding gulls leftover white bread after the toaster in the room burned the bread and set off the motel fire alarm.

Roger Winstead

9:40 am
Along the coast at Nags Head and elsewhere, winter storms have added to the long-term problem of severe beach erosion.

Joel Arrington

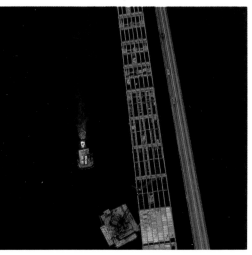

9:50 am
A view of the new and old draw bridge from Roanoke Island to Nags Head, a part of Highway 64.

Ray Matthews

10:00 am

Eighteen-year-old Francisco Vasquez pulls tobacco plants on a farm near Salemburg. One of six children, Francisco has travelled with his family from their home in Piedras Negras, Mexico into the U.S., working in Texas and Florida before settling in the Benson/Newton Grove area of North Carolina. Francisco plans to finish school and become a police officer. "I like doing what I do because you can travel, and see and learn about different states and people. I even learn about myself and the place where I am from – Las Piedras Negras – The Frontier."

Robert Miller

9:51am

Pilgrimage Weekend in Edenton provides residents of the town with an opportunity to display their homes as part of the event's walking tour. Mary-Hannah Evans with spontaneous charm shows that the biannual event isn't just for adults. The two-year-old daughter of Phillip and Challis Evans stands ready to greet visitors to her home, the Barrow Hole House.

Jim Colman

10:00 am

An old apple orchard on a vacated farm has attracted North Carolina water colorist Richard Tumbleston. "Some guys were up here last fall picking up the apples to use as deer bait, but mostly no one comes around," Tumbleston muses. The artist lives on a hillside almost in the shadow of the Blue Ridge Parkway between Boone and Blowing Rock. He's also an angler and an environmentalist, and his best-known paintings are of snow scenes of the North Carolina mountains.

Bob Allen

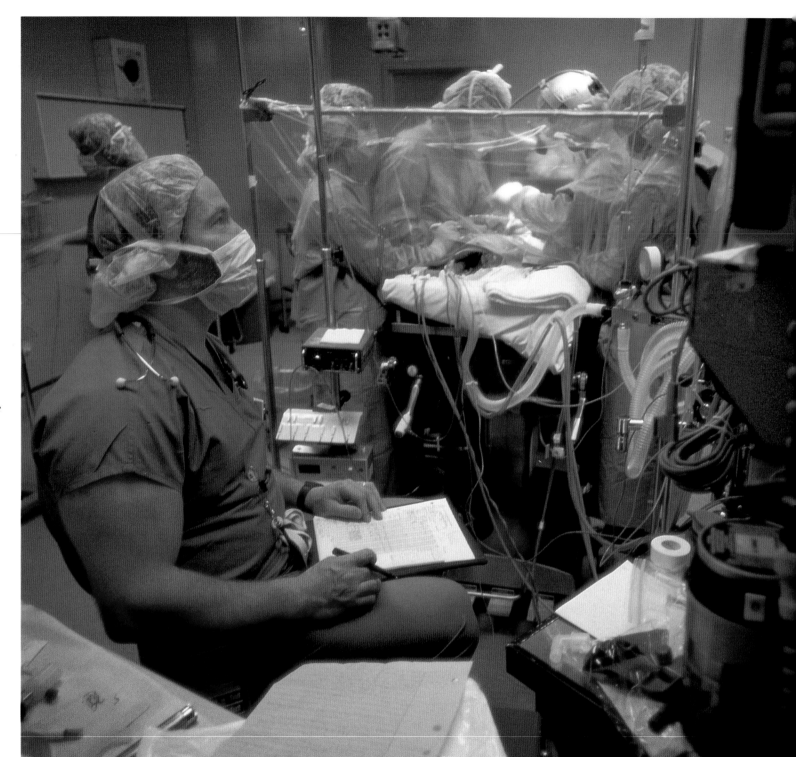

10:00am
Ed Eisenberg, resident in anesthesia, monitors EKG and O₂ Saturation during pediatric surgery at North Carolina Memorial Hospital at the University of North Carolina at Chapel Hill.

Jim Stratford

10:05 am

These are 82nd Airborne soldiers who function as snipers in military training. They use highly sophisticated rifles, dress like the countryside, and are prepared to be the bad guys in any type of combat. These soldiers are SSGT John Figley and SPEC Craig MacMillan.

Ken Cooke

10:05am

Six-year-old Amber E. Crews sits shyly on Chief Henry Lambert's lap while her dad, Jerry Crews, takes their picture in Cherokee. Having posed with tourists here since 1952, Chief Henry is the most photographed chief in town, and has been snapped by pros as well as by dads – for Life *and* National Geographic *magazines.*

Wes Bobbitt

10:10 am
Durham Auditorium with tobacco brand logos in background.

Isabel Levitt

10:45 am
Students and visitors find a symbol of our national history in the intriguing statue of George Washington, the centerpiece of the rotunda of the Capitol in Raleigh.

Talib Sabir-Calloway

10:20 am

MSGT Rich Dunlap, his face camouflaged, is one paratrooper from the 21st MP Company getting chuted up for a jump from a C-130 aircraft at Pope Air Force Base.

Ken Cooke

10:30am

Kate Chaffin changed her regular Saturday hair appointment to Friday because of a wedding she would attend this weekend. Mrs. Chaffin, formerly a school teacher, has been coming to the Vogue Beauty Shop in Sanford, to the same operator, for more than 15 years. The shop was converted from a gas station.

Ed Shenkman

William Faulkner said, "The past is never dead. It's not even past." If I needed a proof of this axiom it was provided as I photographed the communities of Tusquittee and Shooting Creek on April 21.

On one level we see the past manifest in each of these photographs. The way of life that today is the norm in the valleys of Clay County, NC, is enough removed from the trappings (and traps) of late 20th century North American glitz that we can easily extrapolate from these scenes a universal icon of "Life As It Was." The people in these photographs are my pedigree, but they are our lineage – yours, mine, and anyone's who is a native North Carolinian.

On another, much deeper level, I have found the past alive in a much more intangible, spiritual way. My initial motivation for photographing Clay County was that my father, who died at age 59 in August of 1988, had often spoken to me during the last years of his life of his desire for me to go back into the mountains and photograph the way of life that he knew as a young boy.

In Asheville on Thursday April 20, the day before the 24-hour shoot, I stood at my father's grave and realized, or more accurately it was brought to my attention, that my mission in the mountains was not simply to do the will of my dying father. My mission became a personal journey of reconciliation and completion.

At that moment all that I had never known about my father, and all that he never knew about his father, merged with all that I have never understood about myself. At that moment I knew that any spiritual or photographic (can they be separated?) investigation of any one of these three would inexorably lead toward the reconciliation of all.

And it did.

So if all this sounds like so much subjective intellectualization, that is quite acceptable. Understand simply that within the photography I did on April 21 I found within myself a lot that I had lost. If along the way I found some pictures that someone else cares to see that is quite acceptable also.

Charles Ledford

10:30 am

A portion of the great number of family photographs hanging on the walls in Neal Ledford's home in Shooting Creek. Neal's son Jack comments, "That's the way old people used to do; they didn't have photo albums so they kept all their pictures on the wall."

Charles Ledford

Following North Carolina painter Bob Timberlake around his studio under construction in Linwood is like getting a tour of a 10-year-old's room – complete with an exploration of each plaything placed carefully in the toy chest.

It starts even before photographer Charlotte Cannon can get her camera gear out of the back seat.

"Come here, come here," Timberlake says. "Look right here."

He holds an imaginary frame out at arm's length, sizing up a potential picture. He's looking over at the studio, a restored eighteenth century barn, where workers are silhouetted against the sky.

It *is* a good picture.

In fact, most things around the nearly finished studio are good pictures. That's the point: It's as if Timberlake never wants to leave the yard to find neat things to paint. A wooden barrel with rusted rings sits behind the house. A weathered horse trough, big enough for Timberlake to lie in, stands beside it. Nearby is a decrepit-looking shack that's been carefully restored to look decrepit-looking.

It's only a matter of time before the scenes are carefully reproduced with countless tiny brushstrokes – the real-life look that is Timberlake's trademark.

Grant Parsons

10:05 am
Walter Winebarger uses his tractor to spread fertilizer about his grist mill off Meat Camp Road near Boone. The photographer has taken Winebarger's picture at other times over the years.

Bruce Roberts

10:30 am
Renowned artist, Bob Timberlake, is always "somewhere in time." Here he stands in a weathered shack on the property of his new studio in Linwood, which is used in his paintings to help convey a specific time and mood.

Charlotte Cannon

10:45 am
    T. Clyde, son Watts Aumen and farm hands provide a mid-morning demonstration of peach thinning. According to Clyde, "this task is pure drudgery, but necessary for quality peaches." The elder Aumen also spent eighteen distinguished years in the North Carolina General Assembly.

Herman Lankford

111

It's almost 10 a.m. at the North Carolina School of the Arts, and the morning sun is moving higher over the skylights in the visual arts studio. Sixteen students in Clyde Fowler's drawing class are gathering their supplies and preparing to work. Each student selects one of the easels arranged in a wide circle in the spacious, high-ceilinged room. Fowler opens the class with warm-up sketches, and as the students draw he moves around the room, eyeing their work as he walks. Twenty-one-year-old Tony Rogers is a picture of concentration as he draws, his fingers moving fluidly over the paper clipped to his easel.

Two students dressed in unitards arrive to pose as models for the class. They take their places on a platform in the center of the circle, and Fowler gives new instructions to his aspiring artists. "Give me energy! High energy!" he says. He also calls out directions to the models, who must create new poses in rapid succession. The models, Eric Dunlop and Elyse Topper, are students majoring in dance—Eric in modern and Elyse in ballet. The grace and expressiveness of their bodies are clear evidence of their dance training, and one would hardly guess that some of their poses are rather difficult to maintain.

About an hour later in a different studio, a modern dance class is getting under way. In a room with a full-length mirror running the length of one wall, about 20 students—only four of

them male – are warming up for a workout. Guest artist Anne Reinking is running the show today. Clad in flowing black material from her shoulders to her toes, she leads the group through an extensive warm-up routine, while a pianist and a drummer in one corner of the room set the pace. As one watches these dancers stretch and shimmy, the word that comes to mind is control.

For the students at the School of the Arts, a morning like this is business as usual. They are here because to them art is a consuming passion, not simply a hobby or an extracurricular activity. Their ultimate goal is to earn a living playing the piano or dancing across a spotlighted stage. But carving a niche for oneself as an artist is notoriously difficult, and the field is rife with competition. The young people at the School of the Arts are keenly aware of this, and by coming to NCSA they have shown that they are equal to the challenge.

Beth Rhea

10:50am
Two aspiring young artists refine their talents at the North Carolina School of the Arts in Winston-Salem. Ballet major Elyse Topper extends her arms in a graceful pose so that her fellow student, George Lee, can practice his drawing.

Caroline Vaughan

11:00 am

Four Oaks native Dan Lee, a portrait painter by profession, touches up one of his artistic contributions to the town's 100th birthday celebration. "It's my way of giving something back to the town that's given so much to me," says Dan.

Calvin Edgerton

11:00 am

A view of Whitakers, with its local laundromat, hardware, grocery, fertilizer stores and dry cleaners along Main Street, is typical of small eastern North Carolina towns. Located north of Rocky Mount, Whitakers is divided by the railroad into Nash County and Edgecombe County sections.

Michael O'Brien

11:00 am

Clyde Jones at "Haw River Animal Crossing," his home and studio for 10 years or more in Bynum, Jones creates these creatures from wood, fiberglass and a variety of materials. "I get ideas from nature, walking in the woods, trees, stumps...I see things in 'em. I'll just keep turning them around and around until I see what it's going to be," explains the folk artist, whose work has been displayed in New York, Atlanta, Richmond, and Raleigh.

Chuck Liddy

11:05 am
    On Gillis Hill Farms off Highway 4015 near Fayetteville, Jenifer Barnes, Omer Register, Beth Willis and Cheryl Thomas, the pastor's wife, are feeding the transplanter with tobacco seedlings.

Michael G. Edgrington

11:00 am

"Gee, haw, whoa, back, a little more!" These quietly spoken commands come from Jimmy Garner at the Farmer section of Randolph County and are directed at his horse Dean. A Belgian Draft Horse weighing nearly a ton, Dean is 13 years old and the winner of several pulling contests. Jimmy and Dean snake cut-to-length logs to a rough road bed where they stack them in piles for the saw mill. Logging with horses and mules is an art that is being lost to diesel log skidders, but this type of logging is much less destructive to the timber that's left. Jimmy calls Dean "Old Man," but when he easily snakes a thousand-pound log up a steep grade, he proves he has plenty of horse power left.

Terry Shankle

11:12 am

Bobby Gettys applies some patching material to the water slide at Carowinds, popular attraction in Charlotte. He makes a remark that hits the senses: "This ride ain't no fun if all the water runs out of the bottom."

Dieter Melhorn

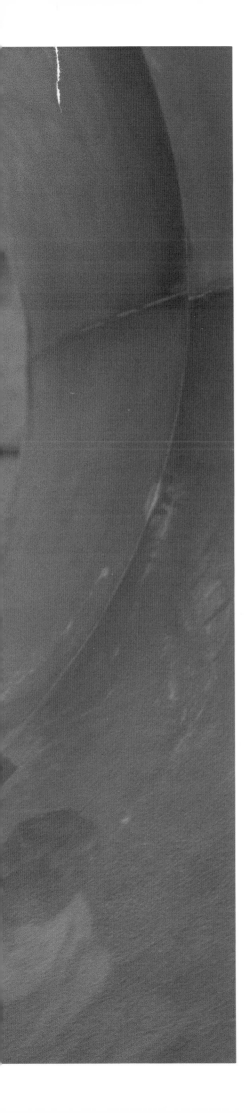

11:30 am

Milton May, 65, a retired school teacher, and James Nobles, 24, a pharmacist, are Pitt County representatives of the international Gideons organization, who were replacing old Bibles with newer ones in the Camelot Inn in Greenville. On a chance meeting, they talked with BIG CLICK photographers about their jail ministry, where these older Bibles will be sent. April and October are "Flood America with Bibles" months. "We're just Gideons and professional men who love the Lord," they said.

Brian Whittier

11:45 am

Flight testing and pilot training are routine business at Airships Industries, Inc. From the perspective of another aircraft, the airships and their facilities near Elizabeth City airport make spectacular viewing.

Cramer Gallimore

11:30 am

An airship at this close range seems not to be too intimidating for W. Earl Farling, Jr. head mastman. This airship, used for pilot training, will be released from the mast by Farling at take-off time in Weeksville near Elizabeth City.

Mark Sluder

"When most people think of airships, they think of the Hindenburg disaster and have the misconception that airships are still inflated with hydrogen," said Stephen Tomlin as he guided photographer Mark Sluder and me around the hangars. We have come to Airship Industries, USA, Inc. in Weeksville near Elizabeth City, as part of our day of photographing in eastern North Carolina.

Tomlin is our host, a training captain pilot from England who has been in Weeksville for three and one-half years. He tells us that this airship manufacturing site is one of only three in the country, and that the hangars are made of wood and measure 170 feet high and 1,040 feet long. The length, then, is greater than that of three football fields.

The airships are made of stiff polyester fabric strips that are melted together with heat and attached to tethers, says Tomlin. Cruising speed is around 60 mph and most are 167 to 210 feet long and 46 feet wide. Larger ships can carry two pilots and 20 passengers in a compartment attached to the bottom of the airship. For take-off, one rotating propeller on each side of the airship is started. The ground crew holds the tethered lines attached to the airship itself and a headmastman detaches the final cable that holds the airship to the ground.

Elizabeth Christopher

11:40 am
Hannah Cobb, 7, from McLean, NY, came to Charlotte to visit her grandparents who have retired to North Carolina. This is her second visit to Discovery Place and the Michael Faraday Show there is giving her a hair-raising experience.

David Morris

11:50 am
   Tom Hall, 4, accompanied by his babysitter, enjoys a sucker at the lunch counter of Hayes Barton Pharmacy.

Simon Griffiths

12 pm
Bob Gilder deals with the trap at the 18th hole at the Greater Greensboro Open.

Thomas Toohey Brown

12:01 pm
Earl Blankenship at the dinner table in the house he shares with his sister, Robilee Ledford. Shown on the table are green beans, pickles, corn, ham, cornbread, strawberry pie and chocolate cake.

Charles Ledford

12:06 pm
Earl Blankenship dishes out strawberry pie made, of course, from home-grown strawberries in the western county of Clay.

Charles Ledford

12:05 pm
At Hayes Barton Pharmacy in the Five Points neighborhood of Raleigh, Mahala Jacobs, "Jake" for short, has prepared sandwiches and other meals here for 27 years, and says of her long tenure, "I've seen babies grow up."

Simon Griffiths

12:20 pm

Samuel Keaton, 71, shows some of the dolls that his wife makes and that he sells from his truck along with his vegetables and fruit. The Keatons live in Reedy Creek; the photographer found Mr. Keaton in Lexington. The dolls range in price from $10.00 for small ones to $70.00 for large ones.

Scott Hoffmann

12:30 pm

Robert Bushyhead, a principal player in the outdoor drama, "Unto These Hills," for 15 years, is working on a grammar book on the Cherokee language. He is a minister and social worker, and an intriguing speaker. Bushyhead finished high school, then college 30 years after his 8th grade year.

Mark Wagoner

1:00 pm
Off Highway 158 near Walkerton, George East runs a truck farm. A former tool and dye maker, East likes to hunt rabbits.

Chip Henderson

1:00 pm

Twenty-two-year old Gary Taylor, a ballet major, stretches in front of a mural outside a dance studio at the North Carolina School of the Arts in Winston-Salem. Taylor, who averages four hours of rehearsals a day in addition to classes, says he chose ballet for the challenge. "It's probably the most demanding, the hardest to conquer," he says.

Caroline Vaughan

137

1:30 pm
    Bob Gaston fashioned this fiberglass sculptured pig on top of Crook's Corner Restaurant, Chapel Hill.

Artie Dixon

1:30 pm

    Fran Farrell has been providing curb service for Wilmington's Merritt's Burger House for six years. Only $6.00 of that $20.00 was needed for two cheeseburgers, two chocolate shakes, an order of fries and tip.

Freda Wilkins

1:45 pm

"We're going to put the AE through the wringer now," is the attitude of the moment at Loeffler, Ketchum, Mountjoy Advertising, largest agency in Charlotte. Work on a big campaign involves (from left) John Ketchum, account executive and partner; Jim Mountjoy, creative director and partner; Gordon Smith, art director; and (reclining) writer Laura Thomasson.

Mitchell Kearney

1:30 pm
Peanut sorting – all dark or imperfect nuts are picked out by hand. Those that pass through go into hoppers for final packaging at Seabrook Blanching Corp., Edenton. These workers (from front to back) are Ruth Matthews, Sadie Whidbee, Ruby Lynch, Edna Basnight, Harriet C. Bailey, and Shirley Ashley.

Mary Beth McAuley

1:45 pm

The Blue Angels performed at the Marine Corps Air Station at Cherry Point April 21 in one of their 40 shows per year. The seven F/A-18 Hornet aircraft are piloted by Navy men except for one Marine. At speeds nearly twice the speed of sound, they are an audience-thrilling act and a good recruitment tool for the military.

John Payne

1:45 pm

Argie Harris, 82, at work in her home in Beaufort County. Of her quiet labor she says, "I guarantee I've graded 20 barns of tobacco for less work than's in this quilt." Mrs. Harris' husband was a grain farmer until his death in 1987. She is a former schoolteacher who listens to "Tennessee Ernie Ford when I'm quilting sometime if I feel real good."

Warren Williams

2:00 pm

Neal Ledford, who turned 89 on April 16, 1989, in the house he built in Shooting Creek community, Clay County, for his wife and himself in about 1946. From his chair Neal faces the front door of the house and the mountains that he used to roam. He also has a view of the road that runs past his house about 200 yards away. "If you drive by, stop. If you can't stop, wave. If you can't wave, toot the horn. If you can't toot the horn, then forget it," he says. Over the years, Neal made his living as a logger, a moonshiner, and a preacher. He always has been and "always will be" a staunch Republican. Behind him are images of Jesus Christ and Richard Nixon. Says Jack Ledford, one of Neal's sons, "I guess daddy thought about as much of Nixon as he did Jesus."

Charles Ledford

2:00 pm
   In Newton Grove, Mexican migrant worker Matias Vasquez, Sr. (Ollie shirt), Antonio Trevino, and Martias' son Lucio shoot pool after working in the tobacco fields of John Spell.

Robert Miller

2:00 pm
   The hand-lettered sign on the door reads: "haircuts $5.00. Why pay more?" At the Burgess King Cotten (sic) Barber Shop in Greensboro, R.R. Burgess boasts, "I may be gettin' on in years, but that don't mean I'm behind the times. I keep up with the styles." Burgess has seen a lot of styles come and go during his 47 years at 117 E. Sycamore St. In fact, a lot of the haircuts in vogue when Burgess was getting started are back in style today.

Roger Weinstein

2:00 pm
Ken Brugh, 71, of Greensboro airborne in his vintage 1930 WACO RNF open-cockpit biplane, one of only a handful in the U.S. still flying.

Dan Routh

2:00pm

At Warren Wilson College in Swannanoa near Asheville, Christy Browning and Mel Queen are working at the college saw mill to earn part of their tuition.

John Warner

2:30pm

The familiar milepost points travellers to their choice of small eastern North Carolina places at this crossroad of Highway 44 in northern Edgecombe County.

Michael O'Brien

2:30pm

"Homeschooling really begins at birth," says Angie Bryant of Asheville. She regards this as her first official year for Maple Springs Christian School. Here she instructs Benjamin, 7, one of two sons of school age.

Chip Henderson

2:51pm

A talented skateboard rider soars above Royal Pines Half-Pipe at Arden near Asheville. A facility designed also for bicycles, Royal Pines is the only place of its kind for perhaps 100 miles.

Herschel D. Williams

2:00 pm
Rupert E. Cowan,
Williamston Peanut Co.
plant manager, sits amid
the bales of burlap bags
waiting to be filled with
peanut seed.

Mary Beth McAuley

2:10 pm

At the North Carolina Museum of Art in Raleigh, Will Brown "in-paints" a section of a 300-year-old portrait, destined for a show at the Mary Duke Biddle Gallery. Since oils darken with age, and "this painting is so old, it's as dark as it's going to get!" (Brown), he'll use acrylics for the touch-up restoration. A special lacquer over the original oils protects it and also allows the acrylics to adhere to the surface.

Merry Moor Winnett

2:20 pm
   A hostess at Duke Chapel on Duke University campus in Durham summed up the prevailing effect for first-time visitors, "Nobody comes through the door without a gasp."

Bob Boyd

153

2:30 pm
Gardner Hudson, owner of Hudson Air Service and an airplane pilot for 20 years, sprays a pesticide on a wheat field in Elizabeth City.

Mark Sluder

2:22 pm

Gerry Mobley washes a Porsche 930S at Quality Detail Shop, Cary. Detail shops are popping up increasingly, not only for expensive cars, but for the convenience of working people who simply haven't the time to wash, wax, vacuum and scrub white sidewalls on their vehicles.

Steve Muir

2:30pm
*Lenoir artist Jane
Norman at work
in her studio, where
her sculptures are mostly
of children.*

David Rufty

2:50 pm
　　The hands of the potter and his creation represent long years of skill and labor. At Owens Pottery near Seagrove, a family business begun in 1910 continues successfully today. The potter here is M.L. (Melvin) Owens, 71. His father, James, began it; his son, Boyd, and daughter, Nancy, continue it. In between, and even now, Melvin is still a creator. When asked if, at his age, he ever suffered from arthritis in his hands, replied: "My hands feel the way they did when I was 15."

Richard W. Smith

3:00 pm

Members of the Smoky Mountain Quilters Guild have gathered at mid-afternoon to compare some of their latest efforts in this charming craft. Shown at the out-buildings of the 1863 Bryson House in Cowee community of Macon County are, from left, Frances Bryson, Mattie Pearl McGaha, Margaret Presley, Betty Andrew, Ardelle Baer, Myra Shomper, and Joyce Harris.

Kenneth S. Sexton

3:00 pm
   The pig farm at
Warren Wilson College
in Swannanoa; two
viewpoints.

John Warner

3:10 pm
*Young Brad Pendley
and amateur photog-
rapher A. Pendley on the
deck of the U.S.S. North
Carolina battleship in
Wilmington.*

Richard Sorenson

3:15 pm

"This shot will probably never be repeated," states photographer Cramer Gallimore, "especially not by me." He is flying in a T-34C Turbo Mentor, like these he's photographed. "The speed of these planes just can hardly be imagined," he assures THE BIG CLICK staff later. His UNC student assistant, Leah Totten, rides behind pilot John Young in the plane that is shown on a straight course. Mike Davis handles the second one which is going into a knife's edge maneuver. These fearsome planes belong to the U.S. Army Airborne and Special Operations Test Board based at Pope Air Force Base.

Cramer Gallimore

3:30 pm
　At Microelectronics Center of North Carolina, Research Triangle Park, Sanjay Tandon and Mark Walters, dressed in space-like suits for cleanliness, work at the reactive ion etch machine used to etch patterns onto MCNC microchips.

Jim Stratford

3:00 pm
　Ian Goode, a third-grader enjoys Private Reading Time at Bridgers Elementary Scool in Tarboro.

Bill Goode

3:00 pm
　Winemaster Philippe Jourdain, in the barrel room of the Biltmore Estates Winery in Asheville, draws a wine sample. Jourdain came to Biltmore in 1977 and became the estate's first official winemaker.

Jim Mosely

3:10 pm
　Charlie Jones of the department of transportation snaps Governor James G. Martin with the week's Pages who came for a taste of state government at close range.

Jim Page

3:00 pm
   Effie Burress of Hazelwood, 108, who gets along well with the aid of a walker and two caring daughters, shows a faded photograph of herself with her parents, taken when she was about 20 years old.

Julie Stovall

3:30 pm
    Looks like a bull's eye for Michael Schneider, 12, as Darell Jones, 11, (sitting) and Rich Tuttle, 12, await turns on "Fun Island" float at the Westport Peninsula of Lake Norman.

Bill Gleasner

3:40 pm

Garland Gaither, 78, has delivered The Salisbury Post *on the same route for 69 years. Through that time, he has worn out three bicycles and has taken only one week of vacation. "I'm my own boss," he affirms.*

Charles Gupton

4:00 pm

Antique shop owner Ronnie Myers matches the stare of a stuffed turkey turned conversation piece. Here at Magnolia Beauregard's in Asheville, Ronnie can point a browser to classic and unusual items throughout his shop, a representative portion of which is shown.

Steve Murray

4:30 pm
Rupert Eubanks, Jr. at
Harris & Ferrell Country
Store, Bynum.

Doug Rose

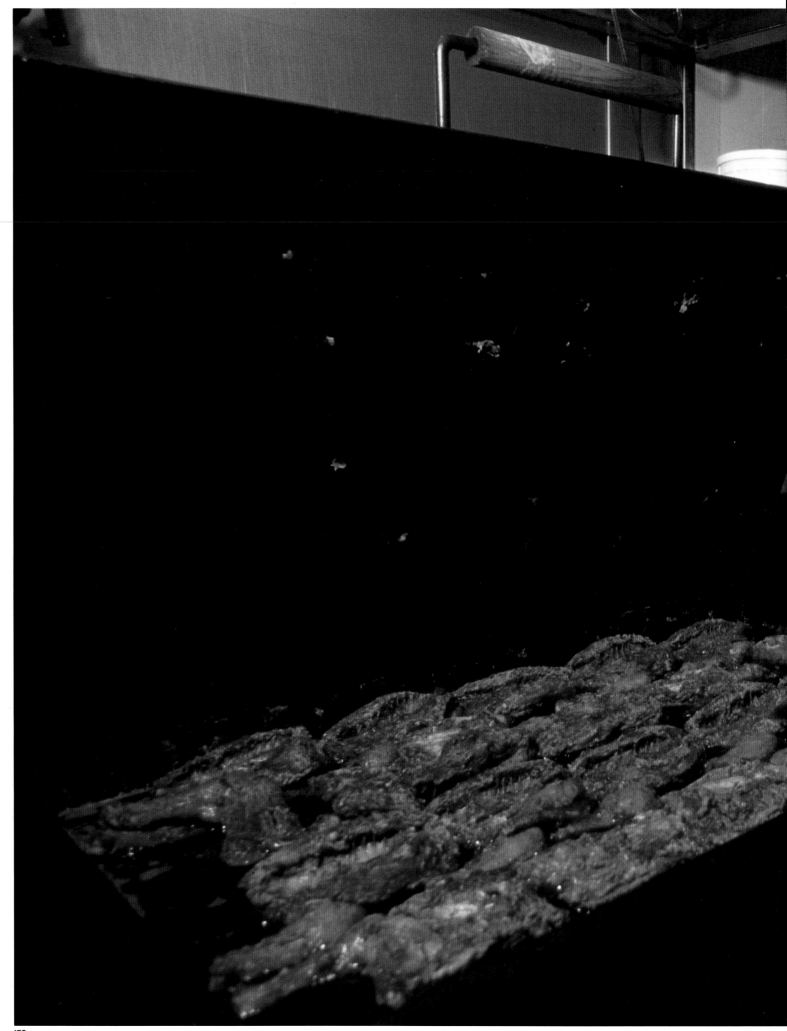

4:30 pm

"They call me the chicken man wherever I go," said B. W. Keaton, owner of Keaton's Original Barbecue in Rowan County. Keaton started his business in 1953 and for 36 years he has been serving his savory barbeque chicken to local as well as out-of-town customers. Even though he is "out in the country," he says, "people come from all over." He attributes this in part to the recognition he has received in the Salisbury Post, the Winston-Salem Journal, Channel 12 television, and PM Magazine in 1987. Most important though has been simply word-of-mouth advertising.

Scott Hoffmann

4:45 pm
    Darrell McKinney has possession of the soccer ball which is serving as a basketball, but Stanley McKinney (in background) says of his own ability, "I jump just like Michael Jordan, just not as high."

Michael McAllister

4:30 pm
   Captain Sinbad cruises through Beaufort harbor in a 54-foot sailboat he built which looks like an authentic pirate ship. Sinbad says, "At first the townspeople were afeared, but now they say, 'Oh, he's shooting his cannons off again.'"

Scott Taylor

4:00 pm
   Darrell Suggs (left), Jonathan Holshouser, both 7, and nine-year-old Rickey Hoskins spend many afternoons playing dodge ball after school in Darrell's yard in East Spencer.

Charlotte Cannon

4:10 pm
   Stephen Hughes, Shaun Mace and Ray Von Dohlen race bikes near Arden.

Steve Dixon

4:02 pm
   Orange surveyor's tape in the community of Cumnock denotes an orderly, dedicated group in Lee and Chatham Counties who, along with Billie Elmore and Max Hall, are objecting to a hazardous waste incinerator which has been considered.

Jerry Markatos

4:50 pm
Compressed by the effect of a telephoto camera lens, a fleet of airliners awaits departure and an incoming plane nears its destination at Raleigh-Durham International Airport.

Jon Silla

4:30 pm

Doug Rice used a Pentax camera with a 17mm lens and remote mounted on the right wing of his hang glider to capture this shot. His camera is facing east toward the mountains of Hanging Rock State Park.

Doug Rice

5:00 pm
  Robin Davenport and Kendall are bicycling home from an afternoon of shell hunting on Bald Head Island. They are on the island for a wedding tomorrow in the Village Chapel.

Jim Moriarty

5:00 pm
    Kenneth Lawrence of Todd fishes the New River near Boone. He uses a #2 wt. 7′9″ Orvis fly rod because of its light action. "Fishing is good all year 'round in the New River for trout or smallmouths," he affirms.

John Walsh

5:00 pm
    Bob McDonough of Wesser near Bryson City lets the rapids shoot him along the upper Nantahala River in the part known as The Cascades.

Scott Duncan

5:00 pm
    Approximately 1,000 buses and chaises are under construction at Thomas Bus Works near Archdale.

Cramer Gallimore

187

5:00 pm
    On Harris Dairy Farm in Southern Iredell County, Lewis Geivais assists with control feeding of newly born calves, some of which have an adoring manner.

Richard Lowder

188

5:00 pm
Claudia and Sesame, two of many goats used for breeding at the NCSU Veterinary School, poke their heads out of the stall for dinner in the trough below.

Kenneth Martin

5:02 pm
*A pastoral setting–
Crabtree Bald in
Haywood County on a
late afternoon in spring.*

Steve Cash

5:00 pm

*Tom Babb of Rockville, MD represents a sailboard company, Blockade Runner Sailing Center, and was in North Carolina for a couple of days. "North Carolina is a windsurfing paradise; the sounds are calm but there is always a breeze,"
says Tom.*

Bill Russ

5:30 pm

Kids line up early at the Rialto Theatre in Raleigh to enjoy Melissa Etheridge in concert.

Simon Griffiths

5:30 pm

Canning done by Muriel Blankenship in a small community in Clay County. Muriel cans peaches, tomatoes, beans, beef, fruit, sausage, apple sauce and other foods.

Charles Ledford

5:38 pm

April 21 was a rehearsal date for re-enactment of a significant Civil War surrender in April, 1865, at Bennett Place State Historic Site, Durham. Ned Durham portrays a first sergeant of the 26th North Carolina Troops.

John Wigmore

5:00 pm

Hugh Harris married in the early 1930's and bought his first car about that time, used, for $290. He and his wife, Mary Elizabeth, have taken care of each other and their 1931 Model A Ford Victoria Coupe. Mr. Harris says, "It was stored for 19 years and has never been left out overnight."

Henry Mills

5:30 pm
Jessie and Melissa Dean at the old school house behind Mast General Store, Valle Crucis.

Bruce Roberts

6:05 pm
The tiny village on Portsmouth Island lies across from Ocracoke, unpeopled, except when open for touring.

Ray Matthews

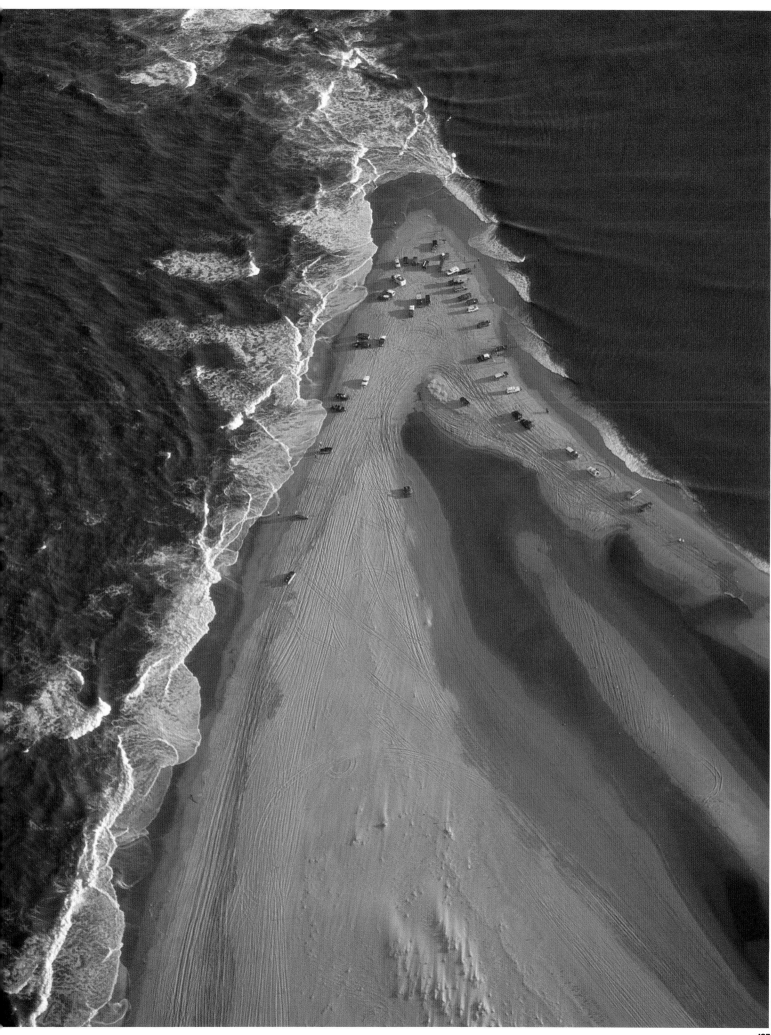

6:00 pm
*A sweep over Hatteras,
right out to the point,
indicates that the
fishermen are pulling in
the usual generous haul.*

Ray Matthews

6:00 pm
*Angel Brooks and
Hezekia Harper at Mr.
Harper's grocery store
and barber shop in
Maysville.*

John F. McQuade, M.D.

6:05 pm
Hezekiah Harper

John F. McQuade, M.D.

6:15 pm

The sun claims only the tops of tracks and boxcars in Spencer Yard, north of Salisbury. For most workers the day is over, but the formation of new trains continues here. Railway cars roll down a "hump" and are connected to a new train at the bottom of the incline.

John Schneider

6:20 pm

The Linn Cove Viaduct, as it curves gracefully along as part of the Blue Ridge Parkway, is generally agreed to be as much an enhancement to the treasured mountain environment as any road could be. It won national awards for its beauty and design, even before it first opened for traffic in September, 1987.

Terry Taylor

6:00 pm

Above ground in pendulum-swing mode is Megan Partin. On her family's farm north of Enfield in Halifax County, five-year-old Meagan is sometimes found even more elevated: riding on the back of a pony.

Michael O'Brien

6:00 pm

More than 100 residents of historic Edenton gather in period costumes for this portrait in front of their city's oldest building, the Cupola House. Built in 1725, the former home is a national historic landmark.

Jim Colman

6:30 pm

Director David Ariail and actors Wayne Webb (center) and Jim Butler run through their lines for a new play in production entitled "Greater Tuna" at Richmond Community Theatre in Rockingham.

Charles Sauls

6:00 pm

A ground worker on American Airlines' International flight to Paris, #767, with containerized baggage in the foreground at RDU.

Jon Silla

6:30 pm

*John Gillis drives a
tractor at Gillis Hill
Farms near Fayetteville.
The Gillis' Farm is one of
the largest family-owned
and operated farms in the
state. John and his two
sons are partners, and
other family members
help in the huge task of
crop farming.*

Michael G. Edrington

6:50 pm
It looks good for Charlie Hamm, who has recently begun pitching. Harry Osborne gives pointers in the Pony League tryouts for thirteen- and fourteen-year-olds in Stokesdale.

Chip Henderson

6:30 pm
Aspiring catcher Kevin Benfield watches his father as he coaches batting practice. Too young for the team of seven and eight-year-olds, Kevin, 5, serves as ball boy, chasing the foul pops that roll down the hill behind him. He attends Winterfield School, Charlotte.

Meredith Hebden

6:30 pm
The cemetery at Bethelberry Baptist Church in Shooting Creek community is the burial site of more than a dozen Ledfords.

Charles Ledford

7:00 pm
    Mark Greene, 16, of Durham, serves as one of the bat boys for the Durham Bulls and helps out by raking the bases paths before the game. The Bulls later win this game easily; 13–2 against the Peninsula Pilots from Virginia.

Jay Anthony

6:54 pm
    Bulls' employee Bob Burtman with the Bull at Durham Athletic Park. The Bull was constructed by motion picture production personnel especially for the filming of the movie, "Bull Durham."

Jay Anthony

7:00 pm

Mike Saieed has lived on Wrightsville Beach for more than 20 years, and although he works in Wilmington for an engineering firm, he still enjoys the marsh any time. "The sounds and marshes are the cradle of the ocean. With a little experience, you can find dinner out here." Mike "found" a two-pound flounder on this occasion.

Bill Russ

7:00 pm
Harry (Johnson) the Clown, popular with children and a true lover of the circus, is in Clinton with the Great American Circus. The circus is Florida-based; Harry is from Sarasota.

Pam Royal

7:02 pm

A third-generation business in Wilson means great hot dogs to customers in the area. Lee John Gliarmis (left), and Socrates Dick ("Soc") join father Lee S. Gliarmis who shows off a sample. Lee S. Gliarmis' father founded the restaurant in 1921.

Brian Whittier

7:14pm

Fourteen sets of look-alikes from the Wilson Mother of Twins Club made it into this shot. Standing, but not necessarily in perfect order, from left are Geraldine Coleman and Josephine Ellis, 42; Tod and Carl Proctor, 20; Beth Rabil with sons Michael and Joseph, 15 months; Ashley and Kristin Boswell, 4; Nancy Holland and John Holland, 20; Megan and Marie Nichols, 10. Seated are Alicia and Felicia Dunn, 1; Christopher and Joshua Forsythe, 8 months; Jonathan and Brian Harris, 4½; Rhiannon and Lindsey Little, 4 months; Jonathan and Michael Sherrod, 4 months; Dana and Doug Flowers, 8 months; Ryan and Michael Wetherington, 2; and Anthony and Kurt Garner, 6. Not shown are Floyd and Lloyd Webb, 60; Mary and Marci Allen, 22 months; and Anne and Will Robl, 10.

Brian Whittier

7:15 pm
Travelers stop at an overlook site of Jump Off Mountain in Henderson County in the Blue Ridge Mountains.

Janet Huston

7:18 pm

For more than 15 years, Blue Grass musicians have been gathering regularly at the home of Nelia and Wayne Hyatt in Asheville. Says Neila, "We have a group of regulars and there are always visitors. Sometimes students will come from Mars Hill college. And then, of course, we've lost a few over the years. The women are good about bringin' baked goods, cake and the men pitch in to buy the coffee." The guitarist on the right end of the group, Clarence Frady, is shown in close-up, and the youngster in the blue shirt, Aaron Farmer, was the subject of these remarks made by his great grandmother: "You know, he used to be shy, but the fiddlin' has really brought him out. There he sits with his grandpa, fiddlin' away."

Martin Fox

7:30pm
    *Ugo Conti and Betty
Sylliaasen show their
abilities at the National
Whistling Convention at
Greenhill Country Club,
Louisburg.*

Wendy Walsh

7:37 pm
   One thousand feet over Runway Five Left, at Raleigh-Durham International Airport, as a train of American Airlines' planes is the last out before dark.

Georg Bower

7:05 pm
   Paul Gonzalez, 39, comes to the neighborhood amusement center in Edneyville on weekends. One of a great number of Mexican farm workers in the state, Gonzalez has lived in Edneyville since 1979, working 10-hour days that include pruning trees and spraying gardens. "I like the mountains better than anything else," says Gonzalez when comparing Edneyville to other areas of North Carolina. "A lot of the mountains here remind you of Mexico."

Scott Hoffmann

7:48 pm
*Travelling Highway
1001 between Denton
and Farmer in Randolph
County.*

Eric Young

8:00 pm
About an hour's drive north of Asheville, on 500 acres of Blue Ridge mountain land, the internationally-known Penland School welcomes the best craft artists of the world who conduct classes for people from practically everywhere. All through the day and night, the creative energies of these artists are directed toward objects of clay, fiber, glass, iron, metals, paper, film and wood.

Judy Nemeth

8:00 pm
The Asheville skyline as seen from the east.

John Warner

8:05 pm
    The sun sets behind Greensboro Youth Council Carnival, which was held in the Coliseum parking lot from April 18-23. More than 15,000 attended on April 21 alone. Approximately $80,000 was raised for the youth council.

Jerry Wolford

9:00 pm

Seventeen-year-old Vernon Blackman (left), from Dunn, stands with the Mustang he rebuilt himself. His friend is Jimmy Tart, 16, from Princeton, N.C. Says Blackman about his sleek-looking car, "I worked for every bit of it."

Jim Stratford

8:15 pm

James "Snook" Stewart and Gina Howell are on Main Street in Benson watching the cruisers go by. The route is around Main, Church and Parrish streets, endlessly, especially on Friday and Saturday nights. Those cruising drive around town playing their radios and talking to friends car-to-car or at local fast food restaurants. Teenagers come from all over– Dunn, Orange County, Wake County and Raleigh, in particular– to cruise in Benson.

Jim Stratford

8:30 pm
   At the last game for the Charlotte Hornets fans have some occasions for cheering, but the final score was 110–Charlotte, 117–Milwaukee Bucks.

Scott Sharpe

9:00 pm
   Hornet Brian Rowsom, forward, is a first-year rookie who scored 15 points against the Milwaukee Bucks in the season's finale in Charlotte.

Scott Sharpe

9:15 pm
   *"The Hop" ice cream
and yogurt shop in
Asheville is busy on a
warm evening.*

Steve Murray

10:00 pm

A moon-bright night accentuates the Newbold-White House late on Friday. The house, outside of Hertford, is the oldest standing house in North Carolina. Volunteers provide daily tours and programs about the house; much of its brick and woodwork is the original, dating back to the late 1600s.

Jim Colman

239

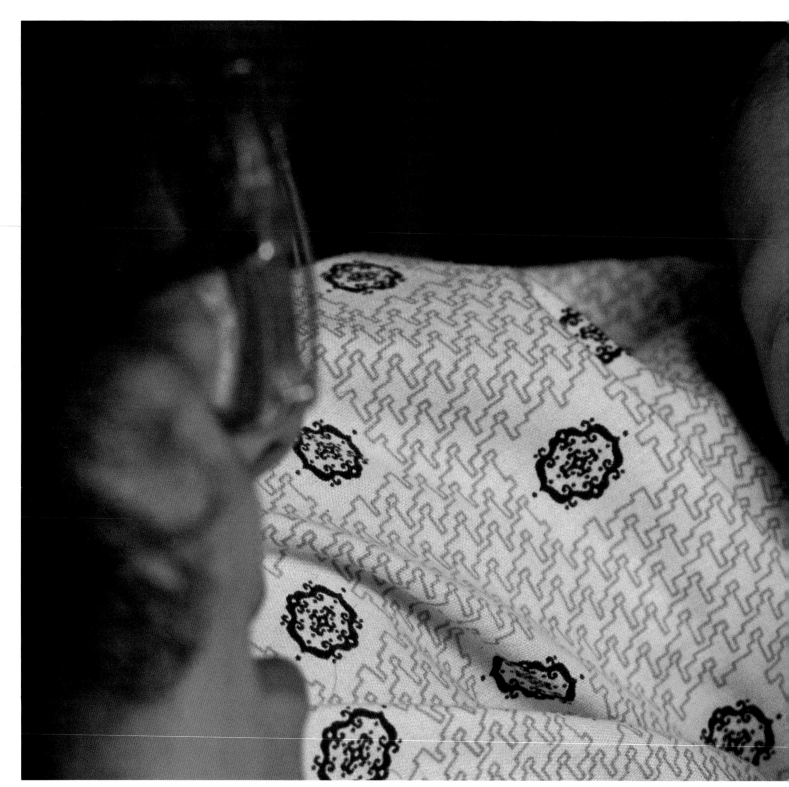

11:25 pm
    *At Rowan Memorial
Hospital in Salisbury,
Amanda Carlisle Stiller,
born at 7:06 P.M. is
admired by her mother,
Cindy Stiller.*

Charles Gupton

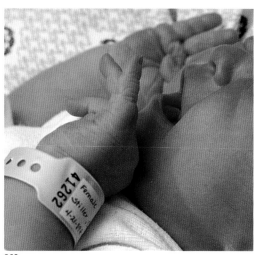

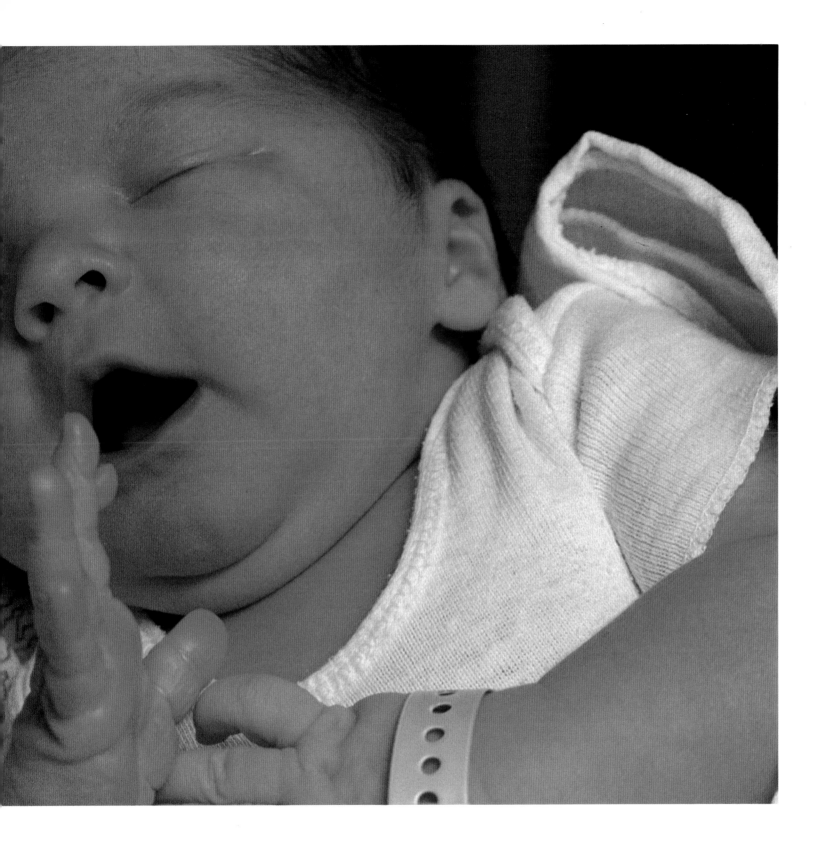

10:45 pm
  "All My Flirtin' Days Are Gone," croons jazz singer Beth Chorneau at the Adam's Mark Hotel in Charlotte. Her trio, called Davenport, features a pianist and a guitarist and entertains Adam's Mark guests regularly.

Mitchell Kearney

242

11:45 pm
*Late at night there
is still light coming from
inside Holy Trinity
Church in North
Wilkesboro.*

Ray Strawbridge

11:55 pm
C.C. Mangum Inc. works on paving the section of I-40 between Raleigh and Research Triangle Park. The expansion is due to be complete by the end of the year.

Chip Henderson

11:59 pm
Dressed in evening attire, these teenagers have stopped for a late-night snack at McDonald's in Asheville, before beginning the 45-minute trip back to their home town of Brownsville. They just ended an evening of dazzle, dance and romance at the Mountain Heritage School prom, held at Deer Park Restaurant on the Biltmore Estate.

Julie Stovall

Credit Where Credit Is Due

Project Coordinator
Chip Henderson

Assistant Coordinator
Brian Whittier

Project Committee
Julie Stovall
Janet Jarman
Genevieve Barker

Editor
Jane Collins

Contributing Writer
Jan Karon

Designers
Annette Simon
David Crawford

Art Assistant
Kathy Shreve Jerrett

Publisher
Capitol Broadcasting
Company, Inc.

*Event Marketing
& Advertising*
The Crumpler Agency

Event Art Director
David Watts

Editing Assistants
Mary Jane Price
Jane Alexander
Rich Beckman
Dee Vuncannon
Lisa Case
Paige Vuncannon

A special documentary
has been prepared by the
UNC Center for Public
Television and Carolina
News Network high-
lighting the planning,
preparation, publicity
and film editing for THE
BIG CLICK event.

Contributors

*Thanks go to Rich
Beckman and the
Photography Program of
the UNC School of
Journalism for assistance
in this project.*

Chocolate Smiles, *Cary*

Blue Cross Blue Shield of
North Carolina, *Durham*

Cellular One,
*Perimeter Park,
Morrisville*

Cape Fear Camera,
Wilmington

Carolina Camera,
Greensboro

Nikon Professional
Services, *Norcross, GA*

Harperprints, *Henderson*

Greensboro Printing
Company, *Greensboro*

Walnut Circle Press,
Greensboro

Triad Helicopters,
Winston-Salem

Litho Industries, *Raleigh*

Com-Tech Packaging,
Raleigh

Southeastern
Typography, *Raleigh*

Camera Graphics,
Raleigh

ADS Printing Company,
Raleigh

Side Street Café, *Raleigh*

Fuji Photo Film USA, Inc.
*Professional Products–
Consumer Products
Division, Elmsford, NY*

UNC School of Journalism
Writers and Assistants

Elizabeth Fassberg
Daniel Conover
Tyler Mills
Mick Stewart
Jodi Anderson
Dawn Gibson
Susan Wallace
Leah Totten
Lisa Stockman
Elizabeth Buckberry
Eric Little
Diana Schaedle
Louanne Watley
Anne Sherow
Beth Domby
David McCollum
Tammy Blackard
Sandy Wall
Sonia Mumford
Walter Denning
Becky Kirkland
Melissa Turner
Shelley L. Erbland
Susana Dancy
Lesley A. Renwrick
Elizabeth Sherrod
Leah Efird
Anna Turnage
Genevieve Barker
Beth Rhea
Elizabeth Christopher
Maria Batista
Scott Tinsley
Karen Dunn
Anne Doggett
Stephanie Bell
Kathryne Tovo
Monica Hancock
Jodi Grabol
Jim Greenhill
Paul Martini
Ariel Remler
Tim Elliott
Malinda Gibbons
Andrea Lacoste
Stacee Singer
Melinda Roberson
Natalie Sekicky
Ellie Lunde
Edward Davis
Bruce Wood
Monica Hancock
David Surowiecki
Tom Parks

North Carolina
Writers and Assistants

Grant Parsons
Emry McKinney
Randy Berger
Eric Marion
Scott Grieg
Jack Haynes
Larry Taylor
Patsy Walters
Kathleen Sharp

Hotel Contributors

Elizabethan Inn
P.O. Box 549
Manteo, N.C. 27954
919-473-2101

Best Western Armada
P.O. Box 307
*US 158 Bus. Rd. MP 17
Nags Head, N.C. 27959*
919-441-6315

Black Beard Lodge
P.O. Box 295
Okracoke, N.C. 27960
919-928-3421

Ramada Inn
*101 Howell Road
New Bern, N.C. 28561*
919-636-3637

Jefferson Motor Lodge
*301 Arendell St.
Morehead City, N.C.
28557*
919-726-7376

Greenpoint Inn
*103 Western Blvd.
on Hwy. 64
Williamston, N.C. 27892*
919-792-4168

Comfort Inn
Executive Center
*151 S. College Rd.
Wilmington, N.C. 28403*
919-791-4841

Ramada Inn
(Old Sheraton)
*203 W. Greenville Blvd.
Greenville, N.C. 27834*
919-355-2666

Hilton Inn–Greenville
*207 SW Greenville Blvd.
Greenville, N.C. 27834*
919-355-5000

Budget Inn of USA
P.O. Box 640
*Hwy. 64 W.
Plymouth, N.C. 27962*
919-793-3095

Days Inn
Rt. 5, Box 40
I-85 at Lake Rd.
Thomasville, N.C. 27360
919-472-6600

Sheraton Inn
P.O. Box 1467
Hwy. 1 at Morganton Rd.
Southern Pines, N.C.
28387
919-692-8585

Holiday Inn
127 S. Cherry St.
Winston-Salem, N.C.
27101
919-725-8561

Sheraton Imperial
Page Rd. at I-40
Research Triangle Park,
N.C. 27709
919-941-5050

Radisson Plaza Hotel
420 Fayetteville St. Mall
Raleigh, N.C. 27601
919-834-9900

Holiday Inn–Airport
I-40 & NC 68
6426 Burnt Poplar Rd.
Greensboro, N.C. 27409
919-668-0421

Messick Real Estate and
Construction Co.
20 Windward Court
Bald Head Island, N.C.
28461
919-457-4717

Lees Lodge
Old Hwy. 16
P.O. Box 21
Glendale Springs, N.C.
28629
919-982-3289

Regency Inn–West
808 W. Grantham St.
Goldsboro, N.C. 27530
919-736-4590

Comfort Inn–North
4924 Sunset Road
Charlotte, N.C. 28213
704-598-7710

Holiday Inn
2400 S. Sterling St.
Morganton, N.C. 28655
704-437-0171

Happy Traveler Inn
1420 E. Innes St.
Salisbury, N.C. 28144
704-636-6640

Gardo's Motel
1134 W. Main Street
Forest City, N.C. 28043
704-245-0111

Comfort Inn
P.O. Box 132
Hwy. 195
Cherokee, N.C. 28719
704-497-2411

Holiday Inn
201 Sugar Loaf Rd.
Hendersonville, N.C.
28739
704-692-7231

Greystone Inn
Hwy. 64
Greystone Lane
Lake Toxaway, N.C.
28747
704-966-4700

Comfort Inn
Hwy. 105 & 208,
Linville Rd.
Boone, N.C. 28607
704-264-0077

High Country Inn
P.O. Box 1339
Boone, N.C. 28607
704-264-1000

Holiday Inn–West
US 19-23 & I-40W
Asheville, N.C. 28806
704-667-4501

Photographers

Lloyd Aaron
Winston-Salem

Todd Adank
Raeford

Jane Alexander
Chapel Hill

Bob Allen
Wake Forest

Gary Allen
Raleigh

Jimmy Allen
Wake Forest

Marty Allen
Apex

Rob Amberg
Marshall

Jay Anthony
Chapel Hill

Joel Arrington
Manteo

Max Aynik
Cary

Richard Babb
Swannanoa

William Blake
Boone

Roger Ball
Charlotte

Ray Barbour
Raleigh

John Barnett
Raleigh

Tim Barnwell
Asheville

Rich Beckman
Chapel Hill

Sgt. Joe Belcher
Fort Bragg

Bill Benners
New Bern

Jerry Blow
Wilmington

Wes Bobbitt
Charlotte

Bob Bogle
Albemarle

Ronny Borton
Fayetteville

Georg Bower
Chapel Hill

Bob Boyd
Durham

Pam Brackett
Charlotte

Sadie Bridger
Raleigh

Jim Bridges
Wilmington

Gary J. Brittain
Greensboro

J.E. Brown
Yadkinville

Thomas Toohey Brown
Raleigh

Charles Buchanan
Kinston

Cindy Burnham
Fayetteville

Charlotte Cannon
Chapel Hill

Ronald Carriker
Winston-Salem

Gary Carter
McLeansville

Ric Carter
Washington

Steve Cash
Greensboro

Robert Cavin
Greensboro

Dan Charlson
Chapel Hill

Mary Eccles Cheatham
Raleigh

Tory Chisholm
Cary

Juliana Ciminelli
Chapel Hill

Tommy Clay
Charlotte

Keith Cline
Concord

Pat Cocciadiferro
Asheville

Jim Collins
Garner

Mike Collins
Goldsboro

Jim Colman
Chapel Hill

Ken Cooke
Fayetteville

Jeff Coolidge
Durham

Anthony Cornelison
Asheboro

Gina Cox
Chapel Hill

Rick Crawford
Asheville

Cathy Crowell
Morehead City

Peter Damroth
Raleigh

Carolyn Dateo
Durham

Robert DiPiazza
Winston-Salem

Artie Dixon
Chapel Hill

Steve Dixon
Weaverville

Bob Donnan
Raleigh

A. Doren
Greensboro

Leslie Wright Dow
Charlotte

Charles Downs
Waxhaw

Scott Duncan
Andrews

Calvin Edgerton
Smithfield

Michael Gordon Edrington
Fayetteville

Ann Ehringhaus
Ocracoke

Patrick Elam
Charlotte

Miles Elliott
Charlotte

Paul Epley
Charlotte

Frances Eubanks
Newport

Nat Felts
Roanoke Rapids

Brian Foley
Chapel Hill

Thomas Forrest
Greenville

Mark Fortenberry
Charlotte

Martin Fox
Asheville

Murphy Frye
Hickory

Bill Gage
Raleigh

Cramer Gallimore
Fayetteville

Jon Geis
Atlantic Beach

Rick Gibbons
Archdale

Bill Gleasner
Denver

Simon Griffiths
Raleigh

Charles Gupton
Raleigh

Lee Gupton
Cary

Cliff Haac
Chapel Hill

Richard Haggerty
High Point

Duane Hall
Siler City

Rob Hammonds
Asheboro

Larry Harwell
Charlotte

Charles Heatherly
Raleigh

Bob Heist
Asheboro

Chip Henderson
Cary

Larry Hoffman
Fairview

Scott Hoffmann
Greensboro

Cliff Hollis
Greenville

Janet Huston
New Bern

Richard Ivey
Charlotte

Janet Jarman
Chapel Hill

Sheila Johnston
Chapel Hill

Mary Louise Jones
Raleigh

Mitchell Kearney
Charlotte

Patrick J. Keough
Morehead City

Larry Ketchum
Raleigh

Lyndia Kleeburg
Raleigh

Beth and Jimmy Kluttz
Concord

Jim Knight
Raleigh

Jim Koch
High Point

Tracey Langhorne
Chapel Hill

Herman Lankford
Raleigh

Scott Larson
Raleigh

Bill Lea
Franklin

Charles Ledford
Tampa, FL

Isabel Levitt
Chapel Hill

Chuck Liddy
Durham

Joe Lipka
Cary

Bryan Liptzin
Durham

Keith Longiotti
Chapel Hill

Richard Lowder
Mooresville

Julie Macie
Wilmington

Stephen Mallin
Raleigh

Tony Mansfield
Durham

Jerry Markatos
Pittsboro

Kenneth Martin
Roxboro

Rozlyn Masley
Fayetteville

Stephen Matteson
Winston-Salem

Ray Matthews
Nags Head

Bill McAllister
Durham

Michael McAllister
Asheboro

Mary Beth McAuley
Kill Devil Hills

Jim McDonald
Durham

Tony McGee
Mt. Holly

Will and Deni McIntyre
Winston-Salem

Tommy McNabb
Winston-Salem

Dieter Melhorn
Lowell

Robert Miller
Raleigh

Henry Mills
Charlotte

Jim Moriarty
Southern Pines

David Morris
Harrisburg

Hugh Morton
Linville

Jim Moseley
Asheville

Steve Muir
Raleigh

Kent Murray
Hillsborough

Steve Murray
Raleigh

Curtis Myers
High Point

John Myers
Troy

Judy Nemeth
Charlotte

Paul Nurnberg
Washington

Michael O'Brien
Whitakers

Tim O'Dell
Charlotte

John Payne
Morganton

Kyle Pearce
Winston-Salem

Richard A. Petty
Pinehurst

Greg Plachta
Durham

Lisa Plaster
Lenoir

Benjamin Porter
Asheville

Marty Price
Concord

Mary Jane Price
Chapel Hill

Bill Ray
Clemmons

Sharon Lockwood Read
Nashville

Charles Register
Raleigh

Perry E. Roach
Asheboro

Bruce Roberts
Irondale, AL

Tom Rogers
Winston-Salem

Paula Rollins
Fayetteville

Doug Rose
Chapel Hill

John Rosenthal
Chapel Hill

John Rottet
Raleigh

Pam Royal
Norfolk, VA

Christine Rucker
Asheboro

Dave Rufty
Lenoir

Bill Russ
Raleigh

Talib Sabir-Calloway
Raleigh

Neil Sander
Leicester

Charles L. Sauls
Rockingham

Zane Saunders
Forest City

A. Mack Sawyer
Elizabeth City

John Schneider
Greensboro

Wayne Seal
Asheboro

Lisa C. Sense
Benson

Kenneth S. Sexton
Franklin

Louis Shaffner
Charlotte

Terry Shankle
Denton

Scott Sharpe
Raleigh

Brian Shawcroft
Raleigh

Ed Shenkman
Chapel Hill

Jon Silla
Charlotte

Jim Sink
Raleigh

Mark Sluder
Charlotte

Richard W. Smith
Greensboro

Steiph Smola
Greensboro

Richard Sorenson
Chapel Hill

David Spear
Madison

Jeff Stark
Morganton

Jennifer Steib
Chapel Hill

Greg Stewart
Asheboro

Helen Stewart
Cullowhee

Julie Stovall
Chapel Hill

Jim Stratford
Greensboro

Ray Strawbridge
Bunn

Karen Tam
Raleigh

Lisa Taylor
Beaufort

Scott Taylor
Beaufort

Terry Taylor
Jacksonville, FL

John Tesh
Greensboro

Bernard Thomas
Durham

Robert Thomason
Raleigh

Shea Tisdale
Chapel Hill

Rex Truell
Thomasville

Sara Turner
Winston-Salem

Caroline Vaughan
Durham

Mark Wagoner
Greensboro

John Walsh
Winston-Salem

Wendy Walsh
Durham

Tom Walters
Charlotte

John Warner
Asheville

Thaddeus Watkins
Chapel Hill

Jay Weinmiller
Charlotte

Roger Weinstein
Greensboro

Brian Whittier
Chapel Hill

Michael Whitton
Asheboro

John Wigmore
Raleigh

Freda Wilkins
Wilmington

Herschel D. Williams
Asheville

Sherry Williams
Kannapolis

Warren Williams
Greensboro

Kerry Willis
Beaufort

Hank Wilson
Charlotte

Merry Moor Winnett
Greensboro

Roger Winstead
Raleigh

Harold Wise
Greenville

Jerry L. Wolford
Greensboro

Jimmy Wooten
Asheville

C.T. Worrell
Rocky Mount

Sherry Wrenn
Hickory

Eric Young
Denton

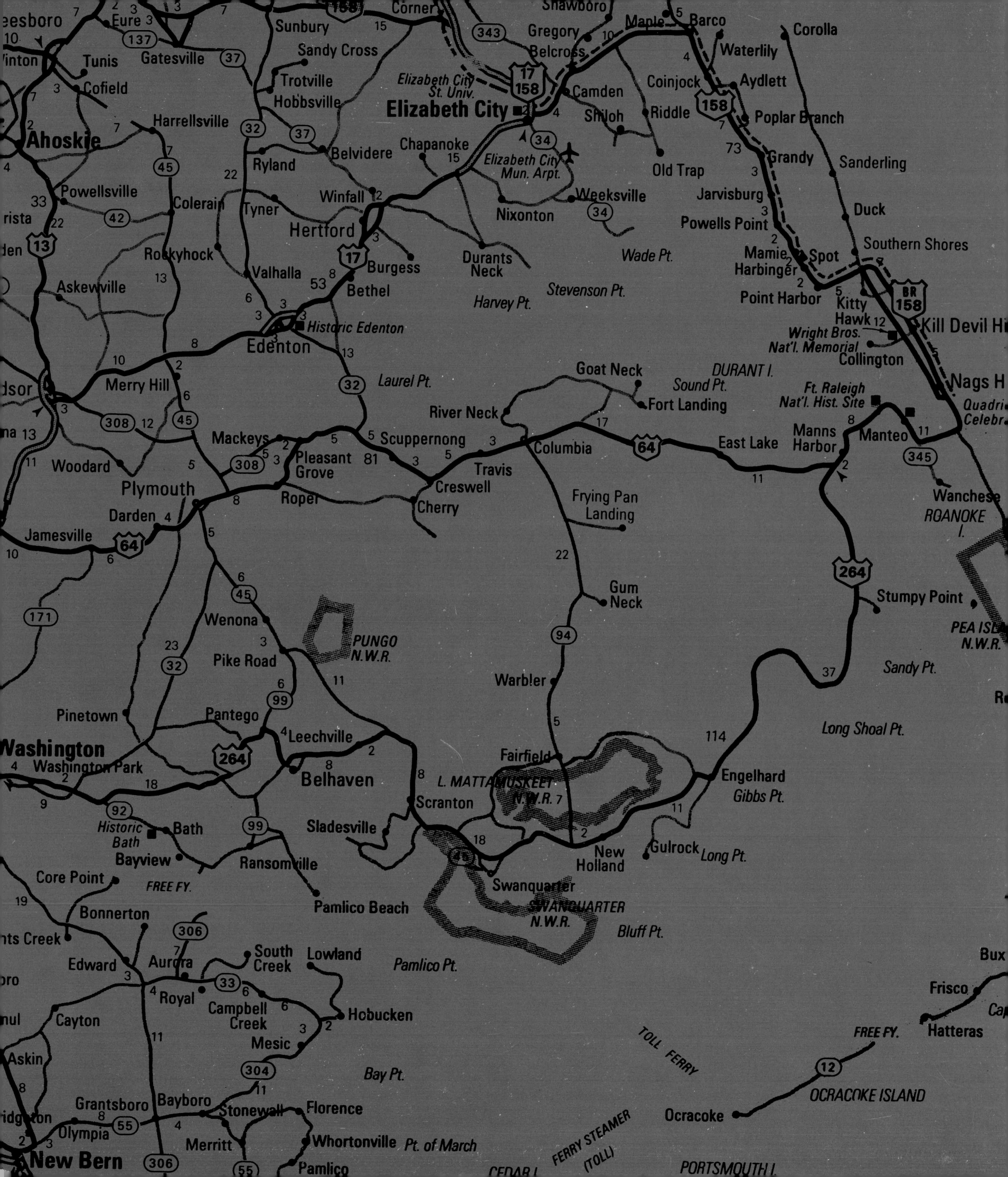